TREASURE IN CLAY JARS

THE GOSPEL AND OUR CULTURE SERIES

A series to foster the missional encounter of the gospel
with North American culture

Lois Y. Barrett

General Editor

•   •

Volumes Published to Date

TREASURE IN CLAY JARS

Patterns in Missional Faithfulness

Lois Y. Barrett, *Editor*

Walter C. Hobbs, *Project Leader*

Lois Y. Barrett
Darrell L. Guder
Walter C. Hobbs
George R. Hunsberger
Linford L. Stutzman
Jeff Van Kooten
Dale A. Ziemer

WILLIAM B. EERDMANS PUBLISHING COMPANY
GRAND RAPIDS, MICHIGAN / CAMBRIDGE, U.K.

Wm. B. Eerdmans Publishing Co.
2140 Oak Industrial Drive N.E., Grand Rapids, Michigan 49505 /
P.O. Box 163, Cambridge CB3 9PU U.K.

Printed in the United States of America

12 11 10   11 10 9 8 7

Library of Congress Cataloging-in-Publication Data

Treasure in clay jars: patterns in missional faithfulness / Lois Y. Barrett, editor;
Walter C. Hobbs, project leader; Lois Y. Barrett ... [et al.].
p.   cm. — (The Gospel and our culture series)
ISBN 978-0-8028-2692-3 (pbk.: alk. paper)
1. Mission of the church — United States — Case studies.
2. Mission of the church — Canada — Case studies.
I. Barrett, Lois. II. Series.
BV601.8T74 2004

277.3′083 — dc22

2004040353

www.eerdmans.com

Contents

Preface

This book has been written by six people, but it is not a collection of essays. Although different people were assigned primary responsibility for various chapters, all of us take responsibility for the whole. We have discussed, debated, and messed with each other's chapters. We have suggested additions, corrections, deletions, and even new directions for each other's chapters. Our discoveries about missional congregations were made together.

George R. Hunsberger, who wrote on Pattern 1, Discerning Missional Vocation, and compiled the sketches of each congregation, serves as Professor of Missiology at Western Theological Seminary, Holland, Michigan. He completed his Doctor of Philosophy degree at Princeton Theological Seminary on Lesslie Newbigin's theology of cultural plurality. An ordained minister in the Presbyterian Church (USA), he has been a campus minister, a pastor, and a mission worker in East Africa.

Darrell L. Guder, who wrote on Pattern 2, Biblical Formation and Discipleship, and Pattern 7, Pointing Toward the Reign of God, is Professor of Ecumenical and Missional Theology at Princeton Theological Seminary, and at the time of the research was Peachtree Professor of Evangelism and Church Growth at Columbia Theological Seminary, Decatur, Georgia. He completed his Doctor of Philosophy degree at the University of Hamburg and has served in educational and pastoral positions in German and North American churches. He is an ordained minister in the Presbyterian Church (USA).

Lois Y. Barrett, who wrote on Pattern 3, Taking Risks as a Contrast Community, as well as the introduction and conclusion, is director of Associated Mennonite Biblical Seminary — Great Plains Extension, North Newton, Kansas, and at the time of the research was executive secretary of the Commission on Home Ministries, General Conference Mennonite Church, Newton, Kansas. She holds a Doctor of Philosophy degree in historical theology from the Union Institute. An ordained Mennonite minister, she has served as a pastor, an instructor, an administrator, and a journalist.

Dale A. Ziemer, who wrote on Pattern 4, Practices That Demonstrate God's Intent for the World, is a senior consultant with the Center for Parish Development, a church research and consulting agency in Chicago. He is an ordained pastor in the Evangelical Lutheran Church in America and has served congregations in Wisconsin and Illinois. He completed a Master of Arts degree in organizational development at the Leadership Institute of Seattle/City University.

Linford L. Stutzman, who wrote on Pattern 5, The Public Witness of Worship, is director of Coffman Center for Evangelism and Church Planting and associate professor of Culture and Mission at Eastern Mennonite Seminary, Harrisonburg, Virginia. He holds a Doctor of Philosophy degree from Catholic University of America and has been a mission worker in Eastern Europe.

Walter C. Hobbs, team coordinator, who wrote on Pattern 6, Dependence on the Holy Spirit, now in retirement in Thiensville, Wisconsin, was on the faculty of Higher Education at the State University of New York at Buffalo until 1993, where he also served for several years as Director of Institutional Research. He holds a Ph.D. in sociology, a J.D., and an honorary LL.D.

Jeff Van Kooten, who wrote chapter 8 on patterns of missional authority, was senior pastor of The Outpost, a church plant for the Christian Reformed Church in Denver, Colorado. He currently is a trainer, consultant, and keynote speaker for both The Center for Generational Studies, engaging ministry and mission issues among North American generations; he also teaches Bible and theology at Denver Christian High School. He is also president of Mazeway, which exists to explore the interface between cultural change and biblical faith. He is a graduate of Denver Seminary, Denver, Colorado.

PREFACE

Our thanks go to the Lilly Endowment, which provided funding for this project through the Gospel and Our Culture Network; to Gail Neal and Penny Marler, who were involved in the design stage of this project; and to Judy Bos, administrative assistant for GOCN, who did logistics for all our meetings over the past three years. Thanks also go to the dozen people who came together at a consultation in 2001 to read the first draft of the book and offer helpful critique. Special thanks go to the congregations that we visited — for their willingness to let us learn with them and share their stories with others — so that you do not lose heart.

So We Do Not Lose Heart

When six of us in the Gospel and Our Culture Network wrote the theological book *Missional Church: A Vision for the Sending of the Church in North America* (Eerdmans, 1998), many people urged us to give some real-life examples of congregations in the United States and Canada that were indeed missional. There were a few who read our book and doubted that any such congregations actually existed. Others just wanted to know more about what missional congregations were like. How would you know a missional church if you saw one?

But many others wanted encouragement in the process of becoming missional. They wondered, What in the life of the church indicates that a congregation is missional? How can our congregation find enough encouragement to continue to move toward becoming missional?

This book looks at congregations that are becoming missional. We do not lift them up as perfect models (neither would the people in these congregations suggest doing that). But in these fragile "clay jars" lies the treasure of the gospel. We want to tell the stories of these congregations "so we do not lose heart," in words of 2 Corinthians 4:1, 16.

The book *Missional Church* was a study of the missional *character* of the church, not just of its mission activities. A proper, biblical ecclesiology looks at everything the church is and does in relation to the mission of God in the world. The church does not exist for itself, but for participation in God's mission of reconciliation. "Mission" is not just an activity carried out by special people in faraway places. Mission is the character of the church in whatever context it exists.

This hasn't always been the way Christians have thought about the character of the church. In Christendom (where church and nation/culture/society were hand-in-glove, and it was assumed that almost everybody was Christian somehow), the church's mission only related to cultures other than the dominant culture. This was especially the case in Europe and North America. But Christendom is dying. Our context in North America is more like the New Testament context of the church, where the church is on the margins, not at the center of society. The mission field is right around us, as well as around the world. We can no longer assume (if indeed, we ever should have assumed) that everyone around us is Christian.

Nor is a missional church simply a congregation with a mission statement. All kinds of organizations have mission statements, and not all of those mission statements are aligned with God's purposes in the world.

A missional church is a church that is shaped by participating in God's mission, which is to set things right in a broken, sinful world, to redeem it, and to restore it to what God has always intended for the world. Missional churches see themselves not so much sending, as being sent. A missional congregation lets God's mission permeate everything that the congregation does — from worship to witness to training members for discipleship. It bridges the gap between outreach and congregational life, since, in its life together, the church is to embody God's mission.

This new project of the Gospel and Our Culture Network began in 1998 with the formation of a research team to look at congregational models of the missional church. Twelve indicators of a missional church (see Appendix) were developed from the book *Missional Church* and from our own experience. Using these 12 indicators we asked a wide range of people across the church in North America for nominations. The eight congregations and one cluster of congregations in this book are among those who were nominated. We make no claims that these congregations are the most missional in North America. But we do claim that each of these congregations exhibits some missional characteristics and is seeking to move in a missional direction. We believe that the experiences of these congregations that we visited, interviewed, experienced, and discussed with each other will encourage other congregations in their journey toward becoming missional. Some of the congregations may be quite different from your own congregation, and we hope that these stories will open the door to learning from those differences.

As we studied these congregations using our original set of 12 indicators, we learned that these indicators were not adequate. We discovered that these congregations corporately spent much time in prayer. And perhaps because of this, these congregations were not afraid to take risks. Secondly, we realized that none of our indicators had to do with church leaders. Yet authority within the congregation was a key factor in the movement toward becoming missional. Moreover, we realized that what we had were not so much "indicators" as "patterns."

Accordingly, we combined some indicators, revised some, and added others, so that we now have eight patterns — patterns on clay jars — of church life that let the "light of the knowledge of the glory of God in the face of Jesus Christ" shine through.

The churches in our sample are not identical. You will find a diverse group of congregations — diverse in terms of geography, tradition, ethnicity, and size — who are seeking to be faithful to God's call to them. You will have "patterns." A diamond pattern on a piece of pueblo pottery may look different from one pueblo to another. Yet it is recognizable as a diamond, and it is recognizable as a particular style of pottery. Similarly, a pattern like "biblical formation and discipleship" may have a different structure from one congregation to another, but it is still recognizable.

So, this is not a "how-to-become-a-successful-church" book, with an easy three-step process for becoming missional. Implicit in most of the how-to books is a theology that assumes that God's purpose in the world is sufficiently described by the numerical growth of the congregation — or that doing these particular faithful activities will result in numerical growth. Some of the congregations in our study are large, and some are relatively small.

Nor is this simply a sociological study of congregations. Dependence on the Holy Spirit and listening for God's unique call to a particular congregation are not patterns that can always be perceived through the five senses or discerned through reason alone.

What we hope you will find are patterns that will encourage you in your own congregation's journey toward becoming missional. Perhaps you will see a design on another congregation's clay jar and be inspired to create a similar pattern on your own.

Patterns of the Missional Church

Here are the patterns of missional faithfulness around which we have organized this book, with corresponding verses from 2 Corinthians 4. As our team worked with these missional patterns and studied the Bible together, we were drawn to this particular passage from Scripture. At first we were drawn by verse 7, "But we have this treasure in clay jars, so that it may be made clear that this extraordinary power belongs to God and does not come from us." These congregations we had studied were "clay jars"; none was a perfect example of a missional church. But each carried in its witness a remarkable treasure that pointed to God's power and to God's purposes in the world. As we continued to study 2 Corinthians 4, we discovered that all eight of our patterns had some reference in this chapter, and so we chose to build our writing around it.

> *Pattern 1, Missional Vocation.* The congregation is discovering together the missional vocation of the community. It is beginning to redefine "success" and "vitality" in terms of faithfulness to God's calling and sending. It is seeking to discern God's specific missional vocation ("charisms") for the entire community and for all of its members.
>
> "We have this ministry through the mercy shown to us." (2 Cor. 4:1)

> *Pattern 2, Biblical Formation and Discipleship.* The missional church is a community in which all members are involved in learning what it means to be disciples of Jesus. The Bible is normative in this church's life. Biblical formation and discipling are essential for members of the congregation.
>
> "We have the same spirit of faith that is in accordance with scripture.... Even though our outer nature is wasting away, our inner nature is being renewed day by day." (2 Cor. 4:13, 16)

Pattern 3, Taking Risks as a Contrast Community. The missional church is learning to take risks for the sake of the gospel. It understands itself as different from the world because of its participation in the life, death, and resurrection of its Lord. It is raising questions, often threatening ones, about the church's cultural captivity, and it is grappling with the ethical and structural implications of its missional vocation. It is learning to deal with internal and external resistance.

"And even if our gospel is veiled, it is veiled to those who are headed toward destruction. In their case, the god of this age has blinded the minds of the unbelievers, to keep them from seeing the light of the gospel of the glory of Christ, who is the image of God. . . . We are afflicted in every way, but not crushed; perplexed, but not given to despair; persecuted, but not forsaken; struck down, but not destroyed." (2 Cor. 4:3-4, 8-9)

Pattern 4, Practices That Demonstrate God's Intent for the World. The pattern of the church's life as community is a demonstration of what God intends for the life of the whole world. The practices of the church embody mutual care, reconciliation, loving accountability, and hospitality. A missional church is indicated by how Christians behave toward one another.

"We have renounced the shameful things that one hides; we refuse to practice cunning or to falsify God's word, but by the open statement of the truth we commend ourselves to the conscience of everyone in the sight of God." (2 Cor. 4:2)

Pattern 5, Worship as Public Witness. Worship is the central act by which the community celebrates with joy and thanksgiving both God's presence and God's promised future. Flowing out of its worship, the community has a vital public witness.

"For we do not proclaim ourselves; we proclaim Jesus Christ as Lord. . . . For it is the God who said, 'Let light shine out of darkness,' who has shone in our hearts to give the light of the knowledge of the glory of God in the face of Jesus Christ." (2 Cor. 4:5-6)

Pattern 6: Dependence on the Holy Spirit. The missional community confesses its dependence upon the Holy Spirit, shown in particular in its practices of corporate prayer.

"So that it may be made clear that this extraordinary power belongs to God and does not come from us." (2 Cor. 4:7b)

Pattern 7: Pointing Toward the Reign of God. The missional church understands its calling as witness to the gospel of the in-breaking reign of God, and strives to be an instrument, agent, and sign of that reign. As it makes its witness through its identity, activity, and communication, it is keenly aware of the provisional character of all that it is and does. It points toward the reign of God that God will certainly bring about, but knows that its own response is incomplete, and that its own conversion is a continuing necessity.

For this slight momentary affliction is preparing us for an eternal weight of glory beyond all measure, because we look not at what can be seen but at what cannot be seen; for what can be seen is temporary, but what cannot be seen is eternal. (2 Cor 4:17-18)

Pattern 8: Missional Authority. The Holy Spirit gives the missional church a community of persons who, in a variety of ways and with a diversity of functional roles and titles, together practice the missional authority that cultivates within the community the discernment of missional vocation and is intentional about the practices that embed that vocation in the community's life.

"For we do not preach ourselves, but Jesus Christ as Lord, and ourselves as your servants for Jesus' sake." (2 Cor. 4:5)

Congregational Sketches

These are the congregations — or in one case, a cluster of congregations — that our research team visited. In most cases, the visit was over a weekend, when we could participate in Sunday worship. We also interviewed individuals, met with small groups, and observed the life of the congregations. (See the Appendix for a more detailed account of our methodology.) The names listed with each of the sketches are the team members who participated in the on-site visit to the congregation. We recognize that many, perhaps all, of the congregations have changed since then. Leaders may have changed. Certain structures may have changed. Information is intended to be accurate at the time of the visits (mostly in 1999).

These sketches do not say everything we learned about these congregations. In fact, readers will find more information and more stories scattered throughout the chapters. Here we want to give a portrait, a snapshot, of each congregation as we saw it.

Boulder Mennonite Church of Boulder, Colorado

Lois Y. Barrett and Jeff Van Kooten

Boulder Mennonite Church is a congregation of about 75 people located near the campus of the University of Colorado. It was begun in

1985 at the initiative of the Western District Conference of the General Conference Mennonite Church. It also has an association with the Church of the Brethren. As the only Mennonite congregation in Boulder, it attracts a variety of people who had been Mennonites before they moved to Boulder plus a number of people who first learned about Mennonites at the Boulder Mennonite Church. Some people drive more than 30 miles to attend worship services.

Although not a typical Mennonite congregation, it has taken the Mennonite tradition and shaped it for its own context in Boulder. The Mennonite emphases on peace and service have particularly energized the Boulder Mennonite Church. In cooperation with the denomination, the congregation has sponsored a Mennonite Voluntary Service unit, in which volunteers (mostly single young adults) are assigned to the Boulder Mennonite Church for a term of service of from one to three years. Several members of the congregation are part of Christian Peacemaker Teams (a North America–wide organization that tries to defuse violence around the world). Some of these are on a local "reserve team" of peacemakers; others are serving in Hebron, West Bank. Boulder Mennonite Church initiated a Victim-Offender Reconciliation Program (VORP), which provides mediation of crimes, especially those committed by juvenile offenders. Mennonite Voluntary Service workers have staffed the VORP program, as well as the Rocky Mountain Peace Center, whose offices are housed in the church building.

One member, David, commented, "People all over this area know Boulder Mennonite Church because they know the Peace Center or VORP or other groups that have used this space. When I came here, there was some group doing mediation; there was a peace center group strategizing about nuclear disarmament, and some other group in the sanctuary. This is the most amazing. I grew up in these churches where everything is locked up after Sunday."

Some members who live in Longmont, Colorado, volunteer in a homeless shelter there and provide enrichment activities for children staying at the shelter.

Combined with the outer emphasis on peace and service is an inner emphasis on care for one another in the church. Through small groups and in other less formal ways, members of the church show their care for each other. More than one person related the story of a child with Down's syndrome born to a couple in the congregation. The child, Decker, had heart trouble with complications. There were meals, phone calls, a real sense that this was everyone's child. Sadly, Decker died in surgery at the age of four months.

While Decker was near death and in the hospital, Rae Ann, an M.D., pulled together a group to do singing and praying and sharing of stories about Decker. The idea took shape when on a Saturday night, the word came that he was in crisis. Rae Ann had gone to visit Decker and his family and drove home from the hospital singing a song. It was a song of prayer, asking God to give her guidance how to respond to this family. Somehow the answer came to her that the church should sing for Decker. Sunday morning Rae Ann stood up and invited people to her house that night to make the tape. Probably half the congregation was there. Marilyn and Gretchen, two women in the church, drove down to Denver General Hospital at 10 or 11 that night. They played the tape to Decker. He died five days later. The experience was meaningful to everyone including those who had made the tape.

When Susan and Steve, the pastors,[1] did the funeral, it was as if it had been their child who had died. Then the father stood up and read the Scripture: nothing can separate us from the love of God. One member asked him later, How could you have such faith? He said, it was the church had showed him that Christ was alive and real during that time.

Eastbrook Church of Milwaukee, Wisconsin

George R. Hunsberger and Linford L. Stutzman

A decade before World War II, a Roman Catholic priest named Joseph Stehling established a "mission church" on Green Bay Road just within the northern limits of the city of Milwaukee, Wisconsin. By war's end, St. Nicholas had become a full-fledged parish of the Roman Catholic Archdiocese of Milwaukee.

Father Stehling took seriously the essential role of prayer in the individual and collective lives of believers. The small mission church he pastored so faithfully was available 24 hours a day to anyone who

---

1. Throughout this book we will refer to clergy using whatever titles (or lack thereof) were in use at each individual congregation.

wished to pray, and he was the person there to open the doors to all who came. Regulars who would stop by at 2:00 a.m. on their way to or from work might call if they could not get to the church on a given night. Father Stehling would ask what they would have prayed about; then at the appointed hour he would go to the chapel and pray on their behalf. It is impossible to know today how he might look upon the recent changes that have taken place in the building that his mission church built. There is no doubt, however, that he would be pleased at the many Eastbrookers who still take seriously the indispensable role of prayer in the life of God's people.

During the 1950s, St. Nicholas built a sanctuary replete with basement fellowship hall (including a kitchen), an elementary school named Blessed Trinity, a rectory, and a convent. By the late 1980s, however, urban decay had overtaken the neighborhood, especially to the immediate west, and the number of both parishioners and dollars was in significant decline.

Meanwhile, in Brookfield, an affluent suburb west of Milwaukee, the Elmbrook Church was growing rapidly, attracting members not only from adjacent suburbs but even from Milwaukee itself. Several of those urban dwellers began to sense there was something slightly wrong with that picture. If God had placed them in the city to live and work, then perhaps they should stay in the city to worship and minister as well. With encouragement from their sisters and brothers at Elmbrook, they spent many months in prayer and in small yet determined steps acted to establish themselves as a congregation on Milwaukee's east side.

In 1980 Eastbrook Church was born. When our study team visited the church we were provided opportunity to speak with a fairly large number of people who were deeply involved in that movement, and it is not too great a stretch to say that for every five people we interviewed there were six or seven stories about those early days! What they all mentioned, however, is that a physician active in various Elmbrook ministries, whom the Spirit of God had especially gifted in proclaiming and teaching the Word, agreed to serve initially as the group's preacher. By 1985, Marc Erickson, M.D., had left medical practice to become Eastbrook's full-time senior pastor.

As the congregation grew, it moved from meeting in houses to meeting in larger facilities such as local schools. For many years, it convened for worship each Sunday morning in the auditorium of Riverside University High School, and they purchased a building nearby which they rehabilitated into seminar and office space for use during the week.

During the same period, St. Nicholas parish was in the process of merging with another parish by direction of the archdiocese, and its real estate was placed for sale. Eastbrook investigated the possibility, understood why a previous "perfect" site had been denied to them, and purchased the campus in time to hold its first worship service in the redesigned worship center by Easter 1996. In short order, the former rectory became an administration building, and the former convent became a resource center with classrooms and a library. Eastbrook Academy opened in 1998 with day care, preschool, kindergarten, and first grade, and at this writing it has added a grade level each year.

Eastbrook Church is unusual by reason of two features distinctive to its setting. Most of the adults in the congregation became committed to the lordship of Christ in adulthood. Many are of Roman Catholic heritage; indeed, a large number attended Blessed Trinity as a child, and not a few were married in St. Nicholas. Some Roman Catholic people who still live in the neighborhood find it difficult to see "their" parish facilities now in use by a nondenominational church, and Eastbrookers are sensitive to those human emotions. Occasionally, when appropriate, reference is made publicly to the men and women of God who served God in this place in former years. In Eastbrook's understanding of the reason that God has placed them where they are, the neighborhood (including particularly the residents of nearby streets where the drug trade is brisk) is undeniably a mission field. Neighborhood picnics, tutoring programs, classes in English as a second language, and so on, are part of the year-round ministry to Eastbrook's world — which begins in Milwaukee, though it extends to Africa, Asia, Central and South America, and the Middle East.

Second, Eastbrook is not in competition with other churches in the city. Those fellowships are considered to be Eastbrook's sisters and brothers regardless of doctrinal heritage or socioeconomic status or numeric size or ethnicity. Visitors from such churches who attend an Eastbrook function are asked to "tell us what we can pray about for your church and how we can help," and they are told to "take our love back home with you."

Since the congregation has placed no emphasis on organizational membership, it is not clear how many persons are involved in the life of the congregation. In two worship services on a typical Sunday morning, perhaps a total of 1,100 adults will be in attendance. Children's and youth programs are extensive. Vocal and instrumental music, drama, dance, and the visual arts all play a significant role in ministries of many sorts for many diverse groups. International ministry, which means primarily befriending people of the many immigrant populations in the city in order to demonstrate to them the love of God, occupies a high place in the church's priorities. A Caring Ministry attempts to be in regular communication with everyone who identifies himself/ herself with the church. Involvement in kinship groups where interpersonal relationships can be initiated and nurtured, some across the racial divide, is regularly and persistently encouraged. Support groups for people struggling with drug dependency, for example, gather weekly. Numerous Bible studies for women, for men, for occupational groups, for internationals, for college-age persons, and for high schoolers meet frequently. In many ways, therefore, Eastbrook is typical of "dynamic" growing churches. In other respects, it could hardly be more different.

First Presbyterian Church of Bellevue, Washington

Dale A. Ziemer and George R. Hunsberger

Who in America has not heard of Bill Gates or Microsoft? Bellevue, Washington, is the anchor city on the east side of Lake Washington in the growing Puget Sound megalopolis. The cities and towns of the Eastside have become one of the premier centers of new technology that is changing the face of the world and was the driving force behind this time of unprecedented prosperity and increasing wealth of so many in America in the 1990s.

As the Eastside has grown from a series of small communities to a city of 200,000 people, so First Presbyterian Church of Bellevue (FPCB) has also grown and changed. Without changing locations, First Presbyterian Church of Bellevue has moved from a small suburban church to a large multiprogram downtown congregation in the state's fourth-largest city.

FPCB could well be a picture of the "successful" church in North America. It is a talent-rich church. When Pastor Dick Leon spoke of his dream for FPCB in 1986, he recognized the church's strategic location, envisioned its reach to the farthest corners of the earth, and invited the congregation to fervent prayer "to hear the Lord's leading so that we do not miss the thrilling adventure that stands before us."

Over the last decade, this church has grown in nearly every conceivable way. Most obvious is the property and facility expansion, for which it engaged in successful funding campaigns totaling nearly $11 million. Numerous programs and ministries were added as the number of staff specialists increased. New members are encouraged to create or participate in small group fellowships, the number of which has now grown to between 60 and 100 (no one seems to know for sure just how many actually exist). Mission trips to Central America and Russia have become an expected part of the church's mission for young and old, as well as partnerships with an African-American church in Seattle, and providing space for an alternative school for dropouts. The traditional ministry of caring and oversight provided by deacons in a Presbyterian church now includes a system organized by ZIP code that keeps caring lay leaders in touch with every member household in the congregation. The percentage increase of membership and worship attendance at FPCB seems to mirror the continued growth of Bellevue, where 3,000 new apartment units are currently under construction.

When people who are familiar with, or are members of, FPCB describe their congregation, they think of many things — the small group or Bible study of which they may be a part, the beautiful new facility, or one of several in a long line of faithful and effective pastors, including the present senior pastor, Dick Leon. But, mostly, they can refer to being part of a large church enterprise that offers so much both to help and challenge persons to live under the lordship of Jesus Christ, become engaged in the cause of the gospel, and reach out beyond their own self-oriented needs to others, both near and far away.

Yet Bellevue is highly unchurched, a striking example of secularism that dominates postmodern America. Six percent of the population is involved in the life of a Christian church. The firm grip of materialism and the concern for having the best and the right things are evident. In this context, Pastor Dick Leon is asking the question, How do we become a *missional* church? Pastor Leon has been challenging the session (the congregation's governing board), his 40-plus staff that includes seven ordained clergy, and the worshiping congregation to recognize that their mission field is both within and around them, that FPCB is a mission outpost to its own people, and that their missional calling involves the witness of their quality of life together as much as it involves service to real human needs and verbal witness to Jesus Christ.

Holy Ghost Full Gospel Baptist Church of Detroit, Michigan

Jeff Van Kooten and George R. Hunsberger

The city of Detroit, the oldest in the Midwest, was founded in 1701 and incorporated as a city in 1815. The population is estimated at 1,015,000, making it the ninth largest city in the United States. Located on the Detroit River north of Windsor, Ontario, in southeastern Michigan, Detroit is also the world's largest metropolitan area on an international border.

Besides automobile manufacturing, the Detroit area's primary industries include machine tool accessories, internal combustion engines, iron and steel forging, plumbing fittings, metal cutting tools, and distilled liquor. Detroit leads the nation or ranks among the top three manufacturing centers in these industries. In support of its role as the Automobile Capital of the World, Greater Detroit is also a leader in research and development activities.

The automobile industry has waned in Detroit, and as a result the city's cultural tides have also shifted. The core city was once the thriving epicenter not only of the automobile industry, but of the urban lifestyle as well. All of the "big three" automobile giants (Ford, Chrysler, and General Motors), as well as some of the minor players in the industry, found their industrial impetus at the core of Detroit. Hotels were built to house the visiting VIPs of the auto barons as well as beautiful homes in the immediate area to house the executives of the combustible industry.

Driving along Interstate 94 today into the center of Detroit, however, is more like touring a three-dimensional historical diorama. Large factory buildings, once teeming with industrial life, are now only shells of their former selves. Weeds are more prevalent than asphalt in the parking lots, and windows and doors are securely boarded to emphasize further the economic atrophy.

Today, General Motors is the only major manufacturer to keep its corporate nerve-center in the area, but has moved its manufacturing to areas further away. Cadillac is the only manufacturer to keep a meager manufacturing appendage there. The city finds its vitality stalled, and efforts are underway to resuscitate an interest in the core area. A recent article in *Newsweek* focused on the hopeful renewal a baseball stadium being built for the major league Tigers might bring, as well as efforts of the city council to woo corporations back into the city.

Revitalization efforts are also coming from Holy Ghost Full Gospel Baptist Church. Located on Grand Avenue, the church worships in the old Packard automobile showroom located just north of the now defunct Automobile Industrial Park. One can easily discern that in its heyday Grand Avenue was truly grand. The houses, now run down, were once stately and aristocratic homes to the executives in the industry. Thirty to 40 years ago, the pristine lawns, the classic American automobiles parked along the side of the houses, and playful children running carefree along the sidewalks were the norm. Now one mostly gets a glimpse of mattresses strewn about on lawns, windows broken, and an almost solemn silence surrounding the cultural shift that has taken place on this street over the years.

Founded in 1941 as a Missionary Baptist church by pastor Henry N. Lewis, the church has an interesting history. The original site, just a few miles from the present showroom, is now structurally dysfunctional. Wooden pillars like broken bones attempt to give shape to the external facade of what was once the physical building for Holy Ghost Church. Discarded condoms litter the surrounding property, highlighting the life trapped there both physically, culturally, and spiritually. But the state of that building did not indicate the missional state of the church. In light of the vision to "love everybody," Holy Ghost ministered life and hope to the original community and continues to do so under the leadership of Bishop Corletta Vaughn.

Daughter of the founding pastor, Corletta Vaughn is founder of Spread the Word Ministries, a worldwide evangelistic organization. Through media resources, Spread the Word has given her an opportunity to plant or oversee 30 some churches worldwide. These churches facilitate the ministry of Spread the Word and benefit from her vision and mentoring. She is an ordained bishop in the International Community of Charismatic Churches. She is also affiliated with the National Baptist Convention and the founder and dean for a Bible college that meets in the worship facility of Holy Ghost. These connections provide a dynamic mix of ministry resources and diversity.

It has taken time for the National Baptist Convention to accept the legitimacy of women in the ministry, but in the International Community of Charismatic Churches, Bishop Vaughn has been ordained to the highest of all positions for that organization. Spread the Word has provided international visibility for her through print and radio resources. The Bible college has played a significant role in shaping ministry leaders not only from within Holy Ghost, but around the nation.

Her very presence at Holy Ghost speaks to the clear calling she has for this part of the world. While in Africa, Bishop Benson Idahosa, founder of the Church of God Missions Worldwide, gave her a direct, prophetic word to go and minister to her own "Jerusalem." She heeded that word to continue and renew the ministry of Holy Ghost Full Gospel Baptist Church. This has created a persistence and passion among the gifted leadership of Holy Ghost that Bishop Vaughn has attracted there.

In 1990 Bishop Vaughn and her husband agonizingly determined that God wanted them to physically locate in the decaying Automobile Industrial Park neighborhood. Buying one of the homes near the showroom began a movement of the church to live and breathe in "Jerusalem." Out of 60 families who participated in the ministry of Holy Ghost, 20 decided to take the risk and move directly into the neighborhood. One elder, Lee Lane, a cardiologist from Wayne State University School of Medicine, sold his home in the burgeoning suburbs and bought a house with his wife two doors down from the showroom. Clifford Jefferson was identified by Bishop Vaughn at one of her rallies in Arkansas to move along with his family to become "resident pastor" to the area.

Such incarnational passion for the community, and the risk taking of its leadership, that stands out. Though other churches might have a flashier facade and more members, few would aspire to the depth of transformation that Holy Ghost has stimulated in this area. Such dedication from its members and leaders for the immediate environs gave the church a reputation as a cult from other churches having a difficult time understanding the vision of the call for Detroit that Bishop Vaughn accepted in Africa. Today, that attitude has subsided as the tangible results of such missional passion have become evident.

The neighborhood crime rate has dropped substantially. Drug dealers are being converted or closing shop altogether on the street corners. Property values have risen and the overall morale on the streets is high. Numerous stories like this define this missional community, but two particularly stand out. The first is the testimony of Coretta. A resident of the neighborhood for years, the fear she felt after being diagnosed with insulin-dependent diabetes prompted her to investigate the church so visibly present near her. Over the course of attending for six months, her diagnosis was downgraded to controlling the disease with oral medication. Subtly and consistently during the next year, it subsided to the point that today she is completely free of diabetes. That healing came not from a special healing service, or to her reaching out to make her condition known to the leadership specifically (no one knew of this at the time of our interview), but from the sheer power of the community of Christ's love in her life.

The second story is that of Jethro, a courageous young man who has traveled a road few of us will ever walk. After years of struggling with his gender identity he began to live as a woman, and eventually underwent surgery to alter his sexual organs. Jethro became Roslyn and began to frequent the Holy Ghost Full Gospel Baptist Church. She was fully accepted at the church as the woman she had become. Unaware of her personal history, the community loved her as they did everybody coming through their doors, but without ever compromising on the demands of the gospel as articulated through the bishop.

As involvement in this incarnational community became more pronounced for Roslyn, she began to be haunted by the identity of Christ and his love for her. She revealed to the key leaders at Holy Ghost her journey to date. Adhering to the powerful vision to "love everybody," the leadership respected her admission and her identity. Over time the love of Christ expressed through the congregation convicted Roslyn that she needed to be true to the person God had created her to be and she began the deep personal change back to Jethro, emotionally and spiritually.

Roslyn boldly fell into the arms of this church. Publicly sharing her story did not change the depth of their love and the extent of their acceptance. Today, Jethro, though physically altered for life, nonetheless witnesses to the intrinsic power of Christ's presence in the heart, and is now living true to who he believes God created him to be.

A rabbi once wrote that God created humans because God loves stories. The stories coming out of this community in Detroit tell of God's joy in what Holy Ghost is doing there, as well as the love God has for everyone in that downtrodden place. The testimonies witness to the fact that members take seriously the calling for the missional church to be incarnational. The risk taking of leadership announces the sacrificial love for the world God came to save.

IMPACT Cluster, Seven Churches of the Reformed Church in America in the Synod of the Mid-Atlantics, New Jersey

Linford L. Stutzman, Walter C. Hobbs, and Dale A. Ziemer

New Jersey, the Garden State, is better known today for its concentrated population and extensive network of highways and turnpikes. "What exit?" is a familiar question there, essential to identifying where one lives in the state.

It was not always so. History surfaces in nearly every town and borough of New Jersey. And wherever history surfaces, there is likely an old fieldstone or wooden clapboard Reformed Church building: Nutley, Freehold, Six Mile Run, Annandale, Neshanic, Readington, Whitehouse Station, New Brunswick, and others. Dating back to the seventeenth and early eighteenth centuries, these church buildings were constructed by brave, diligent, and God-fearing Dutch immigrants. They came to stake a claim in the wild and foreboding New World. Distinguished by their commitment to hard work, industry, and abstention from "worldly" evils, they played a significant role in building the new world.

Today the historic church buildings constructed by the Dutch immigrants stand out as anomalies in the otherwise modern culture of highways, high tech, and high stress on America's eastern seaboard. Many have come to see as anachronistic the pews, the pulpit, the

narthex, and the fellowship hall — and the annual roast beef dinner —
of the traditional Sunday morning church.

Nevertheless, several of these historic churches are engaging in an
exciting yet difficult journey of renewal, change, and most importantly,
hope. Recognizing their changed and changing context, eight congregations in the Synod of the Mid-Atlantics of the Reformed Church in
America set out in 1996 on a journey together toward missional transformation. All 150 churches of the Synod engaged in a similar process
for one year, but then voted not to continue. However, these eight congregations refused to give up, deciding instead to delve deeper, to seek
transformation of their life and ministry as missional communities.

Embracing neither to be self-sufficient nor to merge their ministries, they set out on a journey to work together. They began by making
a commitment in the form of a covenant to support one another, carrying one another's burdens.

The IMPACT (Intentional Mission Process for Church Transformation) covenant was formed around six *learning* objectives, because
"nothing we learned in seminary prepared us for the kind of change
we're experiencing in the world and in the church today," said the pastors (quoted in *The Express-Times,* November 7, 1997). The covenant was
formed to enable participant churches to (1) discover what it means to
be God's called people in a new era, (2) become guided by a vision of the
reign of God within congregational life, (3) demonstrate a new quality
of congregational life that expresses life within the reign of God, (4) become more open to the renewing power of the Holy Spirit, (5) engage
the challenges of modern life with the resources of the gospel, and
(6) equip pastors and lay leaders with new insights, skills, and orienta-
tions needed for cultivating faithful missionary congregations. The
covenant involved each of eight churches linking arms with the other
seven participant congregations and with a missional research and
consulting agency, the Center for Parish Development.

The congregations, their pastors and teams of parishioners, expected to work together intensively for three to four years in a carefully
designed process for congregational renewal. The process integrated
theological understandings of the church as a missional community
with appropriate resources for communal learning discerning, and
with planning for major organizational change. Among eight congregations, one stepped out of the covenant early, pointing to the diffi-

culty and complexity of successful change toward a missional church. For reasons of difficulty of the change process, the complexity of the local church organization, and the unique culture of each congregation, the journey was and continues to be different in each participating church.

The participant congregations varied from each other and included suburban, urban, and rural churches. They were large and they were small. Some were growing, while others were declining. Most were not in observable conflict, but a few were experiencing visible tension. Regardless of these differences, the congregations discovered common realities and shared aspirations. The most important commonality was the guiding question, How can we, working together and learning together, become what God intends us to be?

Under the banner of IMPACT, these churches engaged in a challenging, yet exciting and renewing process. Pastor Jill Fenske, once chairperson of the IMPACT Design and Management Team, reported, "The end toward which we move is to be more faithful and effective witnesses to God's presence and God's Word. The work we have undertaken has been at times rigorous and challenging. Our smaller congregations have been pushed beyond their limits and resources, as we have struggled with pace of our process and our varied abilities. We have asked the hard questions about the 'nets' that we need to leave behind."

Participants became fully aware of the obstacles facing their churches in the goal of missional transformation. The Rev. Brent Backofen, who served as the Synod's Associate for Church Planning and Development at the time, observed, "I am continually aware of how powerful the expectation is in the churches that there is an easy solution to the challenges they face; that is *so* powerful. I am continually being reminded of how much the mission of the church has been co-opted or eroded by a sort of cultural religiosity. On the positive side, what I've learned is that there is readiness here to become the missional church."

Rev. Fenske reports further as the IMPACT covenant bore visible fruit, "We have experienced an emerging spiritual awakening through Bible studies, adult education, congregational gatherings, small groups, worship, and teams. We have begun to recognize how insidiously the culture has entwined itself in our belief systems, ecclesial understanding and our polity. We have begun to return to the Reformed understanding: by grace alone, by faith alone, and by Scripture alone. Reaching beyond our individualism, we have discovered that as a 'body' we are stronger and healthier than the 'collective of individuals' ever was."

The participating churches included:

Annandale Reformed Church, Annandale, New Jersey (John Arnone, pastor)

Franklin Reformed Church, Nutley, New Jersey (Jill Fenske, pastor)

Neshanic Reformed Church, Neshanic, New Jersey (Richard Tiggelaar, pastor)

Readington Reformed Church, Readington, New Jersey (Ray Vande Giessen, pastor)

Reformed Church of Freehold, Freehold, New Jersey (Ronald Vande Bunte, pastor)

Rockaway Reformed Church, Whitehouse Station, New Jersey (David Ruisard, pastor)

Second Reformed Church, New Brunswick, New Jersey (James Esther, pastor)

Six Mile Run Reformed Church, Franklin Park, New Jersey (David Risseeuw, pastor)

Rockridge United Methodist Church of Oakland, California

Gail Neal and Walter C. Hobbs

This church's journey to new life as a missional congregation began at the brink of death. In 1985 the Bishop's Cabinet appointed David McKeithen pastor of Rockridge United Methodist Church. The bishop's challenge to him was to revitalize the church, but his expectation was that David would help close the church with grace and dignity. About 13 parishioners attended worship on David's first Sunday in the pulpit. They mostly showed up to offer their new pastor hospitality and to acknowledge their expectation, even hope, that the church would soon be closed. They were elderly and tired of keeping a dying church alive. Everyone seemed to express a sense of fatalism about the the impending closure — everyone, that is, except for one octogenarian who stopped to talk with David following worship one Sunday soon after his arrival. This woman related to him a dream she had had the night before. In her dream she was told not only that the church would not and should not close, but that she would not die until the church grew to a membership of 45. Thus was he presented with his first crisis at the Rockridge Church. Should his ministry focus on closing the church, as everyone (himself included) anticipated? Or should his ministry seek to revive what appeared to be a dying congregation? He took this crisis, this challenge and opportunity, to God in prayer. He talked with members of the congregation and with other United Methodist pastors and leaders. It wasn't long before a few others in the congregation joined him in this discernment process in an attempt to discover God's will for the future of this church.

Together they came to believe that God's will was the revitalization of the Rockridge Church. But in order to accomplish this task, the church would have to make some changes, some really radical changes. Instead of focusing on death, they would need to focus on Jesus Christ as the giver of new life. Instead of a primary ministry of compassion for the few surviving members, they would need to focus on telling the good news of Jesus Christ in their community. Instead of preaching the Scriptures as a source comfort to the faithful remnant, they would need to proclaim God's call for the remnant to spread the gospel to those in their community who were poor in spirit as well as in fact. Instead of taking care of their own, they would need to reach out to others. Instead of seeking consolation for themselves, they would need to make a radical commitment to live faithfully as missionaries in a hurting world that needed desperately to experience God's love and salvation.

It wasn't long before the character of their worship services changed from solemn assemblies to celebrations of God, before their meetings were reoriented from doing business to renewing the faith of the church leadership, before their vision for mission was transformed from dying with dignity as an institution to living as a community of faith. The first Wesley-style covenant groups were formed in 1987. As people became aware of the changes that were going on in this church, those who were curious about the new life and ministry began to attend worship. Slowly the number of worshipers increased from the original 13 in 1985 to 45 in 1991. The dream of that faithful octogenarian was fulfilled — and indeed she died not long after.

By 1989 resistance to the changes had begun to build. New and long-time members who wanted the church to reflect a more traditional style of worship and service began to talk about how they could arrest, slow down, or even reverse some of the changes that were being made. The conflict between those who wanted to stay the course and those who wanted to retreat continued to grow over the following months. Eventually it became a power struggle between those whose vision of the church was radical Christian commitment and those whose vision was retrenchment in the traditional church of Christendom. Inevitably the conflict threatened to split the church, as each side sought to gain and maintain the power necessary for its vision to prevail. Eventually the District Superintendent was called in to restore the peace and unity of the church. He did so by asking the dissenters to leave the church in 1990.

This was the second crisis faced by David and the other church leaders. The membership of the congregation had dwindled to just a handful of souls, few of whom had been affiliated with the congregation for long. The majority of those few long-term members who remained were homebound and unable to assume leadership roles.

For the second time in five years the church was facing a challenge and opportunity to listen for, hear, and heed God's will for them. Thus began a season of intentional and careful discernment that would last for the next few years. Church members made the commitment to pray, to study Scripture, to meet in small groups, to worship, to orient their lives according to Christian principles, and to practice spiritual disciplines while they awaited direction from God. A vision statement was approved. Three types of covenant groups were set out. It was during this time that they rekindled their United Methodist heritage and began to practice Wesleyan spirituality. In doing so, they began to hear God's call to them as a congregation.

In 1742 John Wesley organized the formation of "classes" within the church. Each class consisted of 12 persons and a class leader who served as an informal pastor to class members. The classes each met weekly for the purpose of mutual discipleship that included encouraging members to avoid evil, doing good, practicing spiritual disciplines and participating in the life of the community of faith. Those who did not adhere to the expectations were admonished; if they failed to repent in word and deed, they were dismissed from class membership.

During their years of discernment the Rockridge congregation accomplished two tasks, the result of which have given them their unique identity as a missional community of faith. First, through the study of Scripture and the seeking of inspiration from the Holy Spirit, they clarified the essential elements of their faith which, provide focus for their lives together and direction for their continuing journey. These faith essentials, as the congregation has phrased them, are:

- Jesus calls us into a discipleship that is deeply personal and inherently corporate. Mission Covenant Groups provide the centering context for our discipleship in the inward-outward rhythm of our sanctification and mission.
- Our first vocation is to be the Body of Christ — the church. To live and work in God's presence, we immerse ourselves in worship and Word, living out our occupations as expressions of our corporate vocations.
- To live as Jesus lived, we are called to an incarnational faith — expressing the reconciling presence of God. We express this as we are reconciled as an intercultural, multigenerational congregation, as we seek proximity with each other to be "salt and light" in our community, as we love and serve our neighbors, and as we form teams to partner other churches in renewal.[2]

Second, they adapted Wesley's class system. Using denominational materials as a guide, they have updated the Wesleyan class system and organized the church into a series of concentric rings which culminate in participation in Mission Covenant Groups.

The outer ring consists of casual visitors to the worship and work of the congregation. Casual visitors are greeted with hospitality and invitations to participate in corporate worship, informal fellowship, social gatherings, and work projects.

The second or "pre-membership" ring contains those who have become more or less regular attenders to worship and are somewhat familiar with the Rockridge Church. The goal of the church is to bring those in this ring to a personal knowledge of Jesus Christ and an un-

2. Extracts in this section are taken from brochures and other documents prepared by Rockridge United Methodist Church.

derstanding of the church's faith journey and its commitment to be a prophetic voice to the culture.

The third ring moves participants into the first level of class or covenant group, the Exploring Membership Covenant Group. The purpose of this covenant group is to aid pre-members in their discipleship journey as they seek to orient their lives to the first "essential" of the church's life, that is, to discover what it means that discipleship is both "deeply personal and inherently corporate." Over a four- to five-month period, participants in this group increase their covenant commitment in incremental phases. As the congregation puts it,

- The first phase includes a covenant to be accountable for class preparation and attendance, to pray for the others as well as for oneself, and to participate in other aspects of the life of the church.
- The second phase commits one to participate weekly in worship and adult education classes, to share one's faith journey, and to participate in a silent retreat.
- The third phase is to continue in study, conversations, prayer, and church life with the intention of joining the church. In addition, the covenant requires participation in the continuing education, mission and administration of the church as well as actively seeking God's will for further commitment to join a Mission Covenant Group.

The fourth ring consists of those who are members of the church but have not joined a Mission Covenant Group. Members can take part in the administrative functions of the church, but have relatively little voice in decision-making processes. Pastoral care is not readily available to members in this ring, although the staff does respond to requests for care. Opportunities for growing spiritually are limited to participation in groups such as Bible study, worship, and volunteering to help others with their service projects. The goal of the church is to either move this group back to the beginning of the process with the hope of obtaining a greater commitment from them or moving them forward in the process to membership in a Mission Covenant Group. It is recognized, but not encouraged, that folks will remain in this ring until they are prepared spiritually for a deeper commitment to God through participation in a Mission Covenant Group.

The fifth ring consists of those who are involved with a Listening Covenant Group. This covenant group is designed for those who are seeking to convert their lives from being oriented around secular values to a lifestyle that is biblically based, Christ-centered, and discipleship-driven. The purpose of this covenant group is to help members discern specifically how God is calling them to realize the second faith "essential" in their lives, to answer the question, To what vocation is God calling me as a member of the Body of Christ? The desired result here is to feel called to either join a pre-existing Mission Covenant Group or form a new Mission Covenant Group along with at least two others who are also experiencing a similar call.

The sixth ring consists of those who are members of a Mission Covenant Group (MCG). At the present time six Mission Covenant Groups have emerged: Children's, Health and Salvation, Community Builders, Youth, Arts, and Adult Education. Current members of the Listening Covenant Group are trying to discern whether God is calling them to form Evangelism and/or Overseas Mission covenant groups. Regardless of its specific service orientation, the covenant of each group requires each member to affirm that:

- Knowing that Jesus Christ, in his life, death and resurrection, offers salvation in this life and for the future, I commit myself to be his disciple. Desiring the gracious initiatives of the Holy Spirit, I acknowledge my need to yield to God. In faith I pledge my time, my skills, my resources, and my strength to love God and to obey.
- I welcome the Bread of Life daily — by praying, reading the scriptures and attentively reflecting on the reading and my life as a disciple;
- I will keep the Sabbath holy and seek to be faithful in the rhythms of my days, weeks, and years;
- I will participate in the central, community-shaping activities of our worship and education gatherings;
- In partnership with my mission covenant group I will develop and exercise my spiritual gifts in building up our church and in serving our community and world, especially the poor;
- I will strive against sin, respond to the warning and promptings of the Holy Spirit, and nurture the fruit of the Spirit;

- Being a recipient of God's bounty and sacrifice, I choose to grow in generosity, beginning with a tenth of all I receive.
- Trusting in the grace of God, I hereby commit myself to this covenant. As we gather weekly for reflection on the Word and the direction of the Spirit, I invite the loving help of those charged to provide accountability.

Each MCG is oriented toward a specific ministry. All of them not only find unity in their covenant agreement, they also believe themselves to be united in their goal of promoting Christian discipleship among member and proclaiming the good news of Jesus Christ as missionaries to the non-Christian culture in which they live and serve God.

- The focus of the Children's MCG is helping church children grow in their relationship to God through worship, education, strengthening families, and mentoring relationships. A second focus is reaching out to the poor and neglected children and families in their community through mission to local elementary and middle-school children. An example of this is an after-school program for community children.
- The ministry of the Health and Salvation MCG is promoting Christian health practices, supporting church members in health professions, and ministries of prayer and healing within the church and community. Healing prayer is considered to be one of the resources the church has to offer everyone.
- The Community Builders MCG is committed to providing affordable housing to the poor in a variety of ways in partnership with a community-based organization. Two innovative projects are the building of low-income housing at a financial loss to the church, and the creation of a "co-housing" development of multifamily apartments, all of which share facilities for meetings, dining, and so on, with at least one unit reserved to house the homeless.
- The Youth MCG emphasizes church-based discipleship for youth in the church and community.
- The Arts MCG focuses on using various art forms to proclaim the gospel in the community and celebrate the gospel in the church. Among its varied expressions, this mission covenant group uses

temporary art sculptures to proclaim the gospel to neighbors and provide the impetus for neighborhood street parties.

• The Adult Education MCG encompasses education and training that builds up the church and reaches out into the community. One example is that of a computer literacy program sponsored jointly with a racial-ethnic community church to train the unemployed in new job skills.

These Mission Covenant Groups are not equally active or successful. The focus isn't on success as much as it is on building up and reaching out, inward and outward spiritual growth, lives lived in faithfulness to Jesus Christ in the midst of a non-Christian culture.

Spring Garden Church of Toronto, Ontario

Linford L. Stutzman and Walter C. Hobbs

To the visitor, Toronto exudes the typical big-city feel of freedom, success, excitement, and optimism. With the Blue Jays, the Maple Leafs, the University of Toronto, a scenic lakefront, glass citadels, and ethnic diversity, Toronto is truly a world-class city. The visitor, of course, does not usually see what is visible to those churches that are close to the city and to Jesus. Hidden behind the human triumph of Toronto are world-class needs. There are also tremendous opportunities for the congregation in touch with the changing reality of culture.

Spring Garden Baptist Church, a creative, energetic, fun-loving congregation in the booming regional center of Willowdale, Ontario, is a world-class church of the postmodern future of North America. According to its motto, Spring Garden Baptist is "Christ in the City."

Perhaps the cultural pluralism of the Canadian context gives churches like Spring Garden the freedom to experiment with their own identity, ministry, and public presence. Or perhaps it is the contagious optimism of the youthful innovators that lead the church and run its ministries, or the Spirit of God blowing where it will, or the ideas of others that fell on good ground — perhaps these all contribute to Spring Garden's irrepressible personality. In any case, Spring Garden is a group of committed, intense, purposeful, risk-taking, Christian entrepreneurs who seem to thrive on the risk and excitement of their experiments and the unexpected leading of the Spirit. The visitor to Spring Garden senses a living Christ in the city.

Spring Garden evolved from rather typical Baptist mission efforts in 1949, becoming an established congregation with its own building in two years. Willowdale was growing rapidly at that time, and the congregation grew accordingly. In the ensuing years, Spring Garden became comfortable and successful in its suburban context. By 1995, however, the charismatic "Toronto Blessing" movement was creating a controversy in the congregation, and people began to leave for other churches with clear positions in relation to it. While the congregation and its leadership were generally open to the gifts of the Spirit, some of the members who had experienced the "blessing" were advocating that all authentic Christians needed to demonstrate the specific "manifestations" that other members found to be extrabiblical and even absurd. John McLaverty, the lead pastor of Spring Garden, attempted to lead the congregation through their divisions over the Toronto Blessing with humility, honesty, and repentance and to allow those who felt strongly to leave without bitterness. While this issue has not been completely resolved and differences remain, it has not been allowed to dominate the agenda of the congregation.

Changes in the neighborhood also began to put pressure on the congregation. Located on the edge of the central business district, the church's land had become prime real estate as the city of Willowdale became a satellite administrative, business, and cultural center of Toronto. With an influx of wealthy Asian immigrants, the area surrounding the church building is beginning to look more like Singapore or parts of Hong Kong, with high-rise luxury apartments for the upwardly mobile, and trophy homes for those who can afford them. Properties adjacent to the church are being purchased by wealthy immigrants, the existing humble bungalows demolished, and fortress-like mansions only slightly smaller than the lots themselves are dominating the suburban landscape. The social atmosphere has changed accordingly, leaving the members of the congregation pondering how to connect with their new neighbors, separated by differences in culture, values, language, and possessions.

In 1996, after 15 years of pastoring Spring Garden, John McLaverty was given a sabbatical, which he began in January by entering the Doctor of Ministry Program at Western Theological Seminary in Holland, Michigan. Through interaction with key persons in the Gospel and Our Culture Network, McLaverty began to recognize that the world and the local context of his congregation had changed and he began to see his role as being "to help my local faith community to begin to make a paradigm shift towards being a missional church rather than a mission church." John's title was changed to "missional team leader," reflecting the new orientation for his role in the congregation. During this intense year of "missional conversation" with the congregation and key visionaries at Spring Garden, the central vision took shape. It consists of two basic premises: a faithful missional congregation is a faith community that is "called back to love Jesus and to walk outwards in discipleship," and is "to be God's sent out people."

McLaverty describes this process: "We recognized that the hardest part was to get the first 25 percent of the congregation to understand these missional concepts. We needed a loose tracking strategy to see whether what we were communicating was not only being heard but was also being understood. We identified six levels of communication in the transformation process." These are:

- awareness — there is something going on here
- knowledge — the facts make sense
- liking the concepts and ideas
- preference — this is a choice we want to make
- commitment — this makes sense; we will make the choice
- buy-in — we are committed to change to become missional

It was recognized that John McLaverty's role would be a "prophetic, poetic role" in telling the story of God, interweaving that story into the journey of Spring Garden, and connecting this to areas of opportunity for faithful missional action locally. John embarked on a yearlong teaching and preaching agenda for missional change that resulted in a vision that was strongly shared by the leadership team and with which much of the congregation began to identify. In 1997 several missional initiatives were taken that solidified the commitment of Spring Garden to carry out its vision of local missional outreach. One was involvement in the Teachers' Strike by opening a day school at the church building for children during the two-week strike. Another was to organize direct mission involvement of members in short-term mission trips. A community prayer walk with 40 to 50 members of Spring Garden participating was organized. All of these solidified the missional vision of the congregation. Today the vibrant faithfulness of Spring Garden is not driven by one person's vision; it is the collective personality of a core group that seems to include most of its congregants.

Spring Garden is marked by a collective creativity and entrepreneurial spirit where the human and material assets of the congregation — money, business expertise, artistic ability, academic degrees, communication and relational skills, time and energy — are all viewed as assets to be invested without fear for the reign of God. It is an optimistic climate that combines innovation with careful, prayerful decision-making. The atmosphere of spontaneity and generosity for the sake of the kingdom has a quality that reminds one of the descriptions of the post-Pentecost church in the Book of Acts.

Transfiguration Parish of the Roman Catholic Church in Brooklyn, New York

Lois Y. Barrett and Dale A. Ziemer

Venimos de muchos	We come together from many
sitios y juntos.	different places.
Aquí llegamos	Here we come
para seguir	to follow
en la lucha	in the struggle
paso a paso	step by step
como hermanos.	as brothers and sisters.
Somos la gran familia	We are the big family
de la transfiguración.	of Transfiguration.
Juntos hacemos	Together we make our way
caminos tras las huellas del Señor.	in the footsteps of the Lord.

The words to this song, written by a brother in a religious order who was part of the parish at one time, are painted on the courtyard wall behind the rectory of Transfiguration Roman Catholic Parish in south Brooklyn, New York. They describe a mostly Hispanic congregation with over 1,000 at masses on Sunday morning and 300 adults involved in "fraternities," groups of 10 to 20 people who meet weekly in homes to hear the gospel, pray, and examine their lives together.

Transfiguration is no ordinary Roman Catholic parish in Brooklyn, where many parishes attract only a handful of people. It is a vibrant, active congregation where the unusual often happens and people say, "That would only happen at Transfiguration."

It happens because of commitment to a vision of the life of the Christian community modeled after that of Charles de Foucauld (Charles of Jesus), a French priest who was a contemplative and missionary in northern Africa and was martyred in 1916. Central to Brother Charles's spirituality — and now to the spirituality of Transfiguration parish — is a commitment to be present with Christ in the Eucharist and present with the poorest of the poor.

The vision was brought to the parish by Bryan Karvelis, who has been priest there for 43 years. He has seen the transformation of the parish from mostly English speaking to mostly Spanish speaking: Mexicans, Puerto Ricans, Dominicans, and recently many Central American immigrants. But this vision is broadly shared in the congregation. Virtually everyone at Transfiguration with whom we talked mentioned this commitment. It serves as a central vision for the life and work of the community.

The leaders of the parish define "being present with Christ in the Eucharist" as more than adoration of the host, the bread of the Eucharist, the body of Christ. For them, Eucharistic adoration means becoming one with Jesus in all things, surrendering one's will to God, being a contemplative. Before an early Saturday morning mass, a few dozen people gather around a simple altar in a basement chapel for an hour of silent contemplation, the adoration. They then pray aloud Brother Charles's prayer of abandonment. Says Anne Pilsbury, an attorney who advocates for immigrants in a program run out of a different part of the church basement, "You give up control over your life." But that turns out to be life-giving. She continues, "Doing this work [immigration assistance] in the context of the parish has made it possible to keep on."

The practice of contemplation is modeled by Father Bryan, who goes up to the church's retreat center in the country on Thursdays and Fridays. Each of the 20 fraternities spends two weekends a year at the retreat center, and the "responsibles" (the leaders of the fraternities) have two retreats a year as well.

The other part of the vision is to be present with the poorest of the poor. On the one hand, this happens spontaneously as Father Bryan or Sister Marcy (principal of Transfiguration Elementary School) and Sister Peggy (who works with immigrants) take in strangers, often new immigrants, to live at the rectory or the convent. Or they go to the detention center and pay the bail for immigrants without papers. Casa Bethsaida, a hospice for persons with AIDS, is in a building a couple of doors down from the convent. Southside Community Mission, which offers social services and meals for the homeless and immigrants, sits across the street from the rectory.

The poor are not just people outside the congregation, but people within the congregation. There is diversity in the congregation — diversity of income levels, different lengths of time in the United States, different national backgrounds. People are encouraged to live simply, not to get carried away with American materialism. "How can you go to Atlantic City to gamble when there are people who have nothing to eat?" Father Bryan asks his parish. He says, "When you concentrate on being contemplative and with the poor, you really do change — your interests, your lifestyle is radically different. . . . I never worry about money. It's just uncanny the way the money comes when you need it. As in the Gospels, it's not worrying about having a purse or extra clothing."

"Poor" is also sometimes defined by areas of need other than monetary. Father Bryan said, "Last week we had the sacrament of oil for the sick. Hundreds of people came, some of them crying. This is what Jesus meant to do — give people strength in those circumstances."

In addition to being present with Christ in the Eucharist and present to the poorest of the poor, about 300 of the adults of Transfiguration Parish practice being present with each other in "fraternities." At their meetings, fraternities follow a format like this:

Gathering
Opening prayers
Reading of the Scriptures for the next Sunday and discussion
Review of life
Group prayer
Eating together

The "review of life" is an examination of one's life under the light of the gospel. How is God working in my life? How is God calling me to life? A booklet of the Transfiguration Parish says, "A Revu is NOT a sharing of your feelings or a chronicle of events & things that happen to you. It is more: it is a serious attempt, through reflection, to listen to what God is telling you through this event, feeling, person, circumstance & where God is leading you." A review is "not simply the sharing of a problem: it also involves sharing your reflection & prayer on it." "The proper conclusion of a Revu is prayer, where all that was said is offered up in general — to God's mercy, love, & grace."

Fraternities provide a group small enough for people to know each other well, to be there for each other, to hold each other accountable. Pasqual and Gloria Chico are one couple who have been in Transfiguration Parish for over 20 years. They could have afforded to move to another neighborhood, but they stayed in the Williamsburg area in order to continue in the life of Transfiguration Parish.

West Yellowstone Presbyterian Church of West Yellowstone, Montana

Jeff Van Kooten and Gail Neal

Traveling into West Yellowstone one cannot help but be overwhelmed by the grandeur of its topography. The nearby Gallatin River weaves itself between canyon walls draped with aspens and firs, interspersed with frozen rivulets of snow encased in spiring granite cathedrals. People flock there yearly on pilgrimages — some to find solace and solitude in its natural beauty; others to enjoy some of the world's best fly-fishing.

Though located in Montana, West Yellowstone borders Wyoming and is the official west portal to the Yellowstone National Park. About 3.6 million people travel through its entrance each year into the rough-and-tumble wilderness — the first to be preserved anywhere in the world. The Union Pacific Railroad established the town in 1908. It wasn't until 1966 that West Yellowstone was incorporated when the population rose to around 500. With the introduction of snow removal equipment around that same time, the winter economy began to match that of its summer tourism. In 1986 a 3 percent retail tax was levied on tourist items that brought in $485,000 in annual tax revenues. That figure has now ballooned to $1.6 million. With the introduction of paved roads, West Yellowstone has boomed to 1,200 full-time residents, not to mention the summer residents who inflate that number to almost double.

The town itself is a confusing mixture of neon signs, outlet malls, t-shirt shops, fast food restaurants, adventure outfitters, an IMAX theater, and a grizzly preserve. Though the financial benefits of such growth are obvious, the longtime residents are in an emotional quandary about what has been sacrificed to reach this point. The quaint qualities of a close-knit small town have now given way to an influx of corporate employees, seasonal workers of diverse ethnicities, and strangers. In a letter dated December 1998, a summer resident addressed the West Yellowstone Church to pursue its need for a larger building, stating matter-of-factly, "Let's face it, West is no longer a typical small, western town."

The stillness of the winter months and roaming wildlife are now also interrupted by the clamor of snowmobiles gouging through the open acreage of the National Park. Such recreational activity has introduced increased levels of toxic pollution to this formerly pristine environment. Environmentalists hate this development. They want fewer people, not more, to visit this 2,219,791-acre park. They realize, as many of the locals do, that this is indeed the last of the Old West, the last place in the United States where the great herds can roam free. Trying to accommodate the hunger for real estate in this region inevitably will change the entire ecosystem of the national park.

Like the Gallatin River, the spiritual dynamics in West Yellowstone also twist and turn along the currents of these cultural changes. Like the complex issues undergirding the concerns of the physical environment, the spiritual issues in this town are just as dense. West Yellowstone boasts four different church buildings within a mile of each other. There is a Baptist church, a Church of Christ, a Catholic parish, and West Yellowstone Presbyterian Church. In addition, between the months of May and September every year, the seasonal visitors bring their unique denominational flavors spanning well beyond the four denominations mentioned. In our visit we talked to Lucy, who grew up with a Christian Science background; Garth, who brings his Calvary

Chapel preference; and others with no specific affiliation other than their own tenuous beliefs and individual search for the sacred.

The major spiritual influence comes not from these four churches or seasonal influences but from the Mormon ward located in the middle of town. Boasting over half of the students in the local school, as well as some of the best summer camps around, the Mormons have earned their impressive predominance and reputation. Though the Mormon presence is prevalent in this small town, it keeps itself fairly insular and out of fellowship with the other churches. In the library of West Yellowstone Presbyterian Church we noticed a variety of apologetic books regarding Mormonism, yet we discovered no intentional engagement with the local Mormon presence.

It is into this milieu that West Yellowstone Presbyterian Church is striving to bring meaning to its fluctuating community. Founded by the Presbyterian Church (USA), the church has been influenced by a number of distinguished guest theologians attracted to the interim opportunities in such a gorgeous and recreational location. After the last full-time pastor left the church in the early 1990s, West Yellowstone Presbyterian Church began to realize it could no longer cling to its heritage or to the town's cultural hegemony to preserve its existence or stimulate its growth. Struggling to make sense of the changes besetting their small town, the membership consistently hovered around 20, the young in the community were nonexistent in the worship services, and the church wasn't attracting the new demographic the tourist industry represented.

This proved to be fruitful time, however, because the significant leadership began to realize a transformation in vision was necessary in order to be a compelling spiritual presence in the community of West Yellowstone. The matriarchs and patriarchs of the church challenged themselves to step forward and maintain the existence of the church, even while discerning through prayer the future God was calling them to. This provided vision and cohesion from the very heart of the church, the soil for growth. Luther, a member of the church for 31 years, told us that God had been "tilling the soil for the next phase of ministry" consistently since the beginning of the church.

That next phase emerged in 1994 and found its embodiment in Pastors Tom and Tammy Letts. As graduates of Fuller Theological Seminary in Pasadena, California, this 30-something team has brought a bit of "cutting-edge" ministry to this small town. Both having served in youth, associate, and senior pastor roles, Tom and Tammy brought a combined 20 years of ministry experience to this task. Though that gave them some pastoral wisdom, it certainly did not prepare them for the full-scale adjustments that rural life and long Montana winters entailed. Tom on several occasions mentioned the mental and physical fortitude that became a part of the long-term residents' character from October to April and spilled over the rest of the year.

This may lend insight into the contrast between seasonal and permanent residents in this town. One group is transient, economically focused, and temporary; the other, long-term, committed, and enduring. These ingredients provide the primary challenge for becoming a missional church in West Yellowstone. Tom and Tammy both sense this and have led the church in ways that are making a significant impact.

Tom brought with him to West Yellowstone a zeal for working with people, especially youth. Tammy brought administrative expertise and a vision for the church's children's ministry. Since the Lettses have arrived, the church has gained recognition in the community for its outstanding ministry to children (around 70 children come to weekly children's church sessions on Wednesday afternoons) and youth (about 30 teens participate in youth groups) since the Lettses have arrived. West Yellowstone Presbyterian Church now sends more children to the denominational summer camps than any other church in its presbytery. These ministries have had significant impact on the families of the community regardless of whether they attend the church. In fact, the youth ministry is the primary reason the church is known in the community. The youth are also well represented now on Sunday mornings, particularly in worship. The service is a mix of contemporary praise songs and liturgical hymns and readings, much of it led by the youth. Pastor Tom has a degree in music; he is careful that songs chosen for worship are rich and deep and true to the person of Jesus Christ. He is also a dynamic communicator. But in spite of all the positives this worship style has brought, they haven't come without some cost. Some of the long-term members expressed to us the pain of losing significant faith expressions in worship and the guilt associated with feeling that way.

The weekend we visited was the launch of a stewardship campaign to raise the funds necessary to accommodate an increase in attendance. From 21 members in the spring of 1994 to 99 members presently, the church has grown fivefold in a short time. Another 50 to 100 people are nonmembers active in the church. There is energy and vibrancy in the pews.

Some growth has come through Pastor Tom's dynamic personality. He has involved himself in the community and has tried to collaborate with the other churches in the area. One person interviewed said that Pastor Tom has "turned this town around," a statement that gets at the heart of the excitement the people feel for him and the integral role he plays in their lives. One concern that unanimously emerged in all our interviews was the devastation that would occur to the church's momentum and vision if the Lettses left. Given the transience of the town's tourist population, Pastor Tom must be highly skillful in interacting with, accepting, and integrating a variety of religious traditions. Many visit the church during the summer, and many others are seasonal residents who attend worship regularly from summer to fall. They bring with them a variety of backgrounds and church traditions, but most have found a real home in West Yellowstone Presbyterian Church. Although he leads a diverse, ecumenical church — indeed, many know it simply as West Yellowstone *Protestant* Church — Pastor Tom has great respect for and involvement in the regional presbytery. He tries to communicate the benefits of such a connection to the congregation, although he sometimes wonders if it really matters to those who are attending. Yet he understands that the presbytery exists for the congregation's benefit, and he appreciates and honors his commitment to it.

Pattern 1

Discerning Missional Vocation

GEORGE R. HUNSBERGER

"We have this ministry through the mercy shown to us."

(2 Cor. 4:1)

Pattern: The congregation is discovering together the missional vocation of the community. It is beginning to redefine "success" and "vitality" in terms of faithfulness to God's calling and sending. It is seeking to discern God's specific missional vocation (its "charisms") for the entire community and for all of its members.

When the Holy Ghost Full Gospel Baptist Church outgrew its facilities in one neighborhood of Detroit and moved to another, it assumed something not many churches assume. The move would mean that a lot of the members would now move into the new neighborhood. After all, they were going to be the community of God's people through whom God would show his presence there. Acquiring the grand old building that was once the Packard showroom placed them in a half-mile-square area along that stretch of Grand Boulevard that had once been housing for lower and middle management in the heyday of Detroit's automotive industry. Now, the housing had become

33

run down, and the area was known for its drug dealing, alcohol consumption, absentee landlords, and downward economic spirals. Families were mostly broken ones. Despair had become the normal way of life for the people who lived there. But the people of Holy Ghost knew God well enough to know that the divine intent was to bring healing and deliverance to this neighborhood, and the fortunes that landed them in this facility were not accidental to that intent.

The founding pastor of Holy Ghost, Henry N. Lewis, had bred into the core of this church a simple, and often repeated, mantra: "Love everybody." If someone crosses your path, or crosses you on the path, "love everybody." If someone stumbles half-drunk into your church service, "love everybody." If violence is done to you by officials or unofficials, "love everybody." And when you plop yourselves down in a community by establishing your worship center there, your new neighbors are the obvious prime candidates for the same: "love everybody!"

From the moment the move was confirmed, the idea of "loving everybody" from a comfortable commute didn't seem to make much sense to the people of Holy Ghost. It was obvious: if not all of them, at least many would find homes in the new community and live alongside the "everybodies" God was sending them to "love." At least half the families of the church did that. While not their original intent, Pastor (now Bishop) Corletta Vaughn and her husband found themselves moving as well, from a more comfortable five-bedroom suburban home to the "Packard" community. (Hearing Bishop Vaughn tell the story of her husband's dream in the night that indicated God was calling them to move — an idea she wasn't ready to hear! — betrays the human realism of a woman who wanted and prized the comfort we all do, while it gives testament to her ultimate inclination to follow what God was indicating, comfortable or not.)

Shortly after the move, Valorie McCune was added to the pastoral team. She brought not only a gifted musical and worship presence but her concern for "Christian community development," a term John Perkins of Mississippi had used in workshops she had attended, and through which her vision had been galvanized. Perkins had become famous for his three Rs of Christian community development: relocation, reconciliation, and redistribution. The starting point was clear. She joined the others, including the circle of pastors and elders, and relocated herself into the neighborhood. If Holy Ghost Church was to be the healing presence of Christ in this neighborhood, anchored as it was in this new worship center now dubbed "the House of the Lord," it would be so as a community of new neighbors sharing life as other neighbors saw and experienced it.

Transfiguration Parish (Roman Catholic) in the Williamsburg area of Brooklyn had experienced a severe decline by the late 1950s. Originally a parish of German immigrants, the character of the community had changed. It was increasingly Puerto Rican immigrants who lived there, alongside a significant community of Hasidic Jews. When Father Bryan Karvelis arrived there, he knew that he was ill-prepared for ministry among poor Puerto Rican immigrants. His first instinct was to seek permission to live in an apartment among them. His own sense of vocation was formed by the spirituality of Charles de Foucauld, which focused on the mystery of the incarnation, how God entered the human condition and in fact took up residence among the poor of Israel. That vocation has passed, over many years, to the new congregation that formed and flourished in the parish. The large, vibrant Hispanic congregation of the present-day parish now bears those same marks of incarnation. Their reason for being is to be "present with Christ in the Eucharist and present with the poorest of the poor."

Central to Transfiguration's understanding of its vocation is the biblical understanding of the Incarnation — God leaving behind power and glory (Phil. 2:5-11) to take the form of a peasant in a land of poverty. Pasqual Chico, a lay leader, talks with tears in his eyes of the wonder and awe he feels about a God who would lower himself in this way. It is this awe and wonder of the incarnation that draws parish "responsibles" (leaders of fraternities of 15 to 20 people each) together on Saturday mornings for an extended quiet meditation, or eucharistic adoration, where the focus of worship is again and again the life-giving and life-saving sacrifice of Jesus Christ. When Pasqual and the other leaders, along with Father Bryan, emerge from the catacombs-like worship space beneath the sacristy, they share breakfast, discussing together the Gospel lesson for the next day's liturgy and the culture of our day that it confronts. Then they share lunch with a group of formerly homeless men who reside at the parish facility, some of whom comprise an unofficial religious order.

Members of our team were welcomed to observe and participate in one of these weekly 7:00 a.m. to 1:00 p.m. Saturday vigils. They came away with a profound sense that this congregation seeks to *be* what it *believes*. Its vocation is to be the living Incarnation of Jesus Christ — to be "present to God in the Eucharist and present to others — especially the poorest among us." Father Bryan says, "When you concentrate on being contemplative and with the poor, you really do change — your interests, your lifestyle are radically different." Pasqual adds, in a way that vividly captures this incarnational vocation, "We are Matthew 25."

The Vocation of the Congregation

"We are Matthew 25." "We have this ministry." "We have this treasure." "Clay jar though we are, the mercy shown to us is more than enough to set us on the path of bearing this treasure." These are the attitudes that lie deepest at the root of what distinguishes congregations as missional. No grand program of success does it. No ambitious activism. No effort to change the world or win it back. Simply the humility of being God's servants. Being a missional church is all about a sense of identity, shared pervasively in a congregation that knows it is caught up into God's intent for the world. It comes from having heard, one way or another, the still, small voice that says, "You are mine. I have called you to me. I join you to my compassionate approach to the whole world for its healing. You are witnesses to what I have done and what I will yet do."

We are calling this "missional vocation." That is not a phrase any of the churches we visited would use. But it is what we discovered about each of them, that they are concerned to discern and follow their God-given vocation, their calling. They live at different places along the way. For some the discernment is a fresh quest. For others it simply happened to them as they tried to be faithful where they were planted. For some it's a very conscious thing. For others it's simply the way they do things. But for all of them, there is a sense that they are here for some reason, and that reason is bound up with the call of God. They are in service to something bigger than themselves. The reign of God has captivated them in Jesus Christ, and increasingly it defines them. The mission of God defines what their own mission must be. Their mission is not defined by some discernable group of potential clients for whom they might provide certain services. Nor is it defined by identifying potential members of their organization, as though the task is one of re-cruitment. Rather, for these congregations it is a matter of faithfulness to a God-given vocation.

Vocation is a word that has gone out of fashion. When it is used, it normally refers simply to one's chosen career or line of work, one's pro-fession, perhaps. In this regard, the meaning has slipped from earlier uses of the word, especially by Christians. For one thing, it conceives of vocation as a narrow band of activities — the work-related ones. Ori-ginally, when Christians spoke of their vocation, the word had greater depth and breadth. In his definition for the word, Paul Stevens picks up the fuller meaning of the conception. For him, vocation is "experi-encing and living by a calling" in such a way that it "provides a funda-mental orientation to everyday life" (in *The Dictionary of Christianity in Everyday Life,* ed. by Robert Banks and R. Paul Stevens [Downers Grove: InterVarsity Press, 1999], p. 97). *Calling* is the operative word here. In fact, the Latin root of our English word *vocation* is *vocatio,* which means "to call." All the ramifications of God's calling are in view: tasks, prac-tices, attitudes, perspectives, beliefs, vows!

The other slippage is apparent when we so easily talk about voca-tion as *one's chosen career.* We may in fact refer to that as a "calling," but most often that is quite apart from a clear notion that there is a "caller." For the Christian, vocation has to do with being called by, and toward, someone! The call of God in Christ orients and governs the choices we make, which then become more like discernments of calling than they are personal preferences.

The book *Missional Church* was deliberate about describing the missional quality of the church as being "called and sent" by God. These are not two separate acts of God, with one as the prior condition of the other, or one as the counterbalance to the other. They are one and the same! For the church to understand itself to be missional ("sent") is to discern its vocation ("calling"). To be called by God is to be taken into a way of life and mission. That is why Klaus Bockmuehl puts the issue this way:

> [Jesus] saw himself as a man with a mission, in the literal sense
> of someone who has been sent. Jesus' goal in life, his perspective,
> had been set for him. They were a divine commission and assign-
> ment. This is exactly what we call "vocation" in the life of a

Christian. Our "vocation" is derived from, and the complement of, Christ's mission. ("Recovering Vocation Today," *Crux* 24, 3, September 1988, p. 25)

But here we are speaking of vocation in a corporate sense, in reference to a congregation, and we believe it is right to do that. For one thing, there are biblical grounds for it. The Old Testament word for call *(qara)* is primarily used for "the people of God who are summoned to participate in God's grand purpose for the world." In similar fashion, in the New Testament the call *(kaleo, klesis)* is "the summons to holy corporate and personal living and the call to serve" ("Calling/Vocation," p. 99).

This in no way denies each person's own vocation, each one's own calling, which will have its unique, particular contours. And of course, it is not hard to see that the collective vocations of the people of a congregation will have a certain cumulative effect on the character of the whole. But we are saying something more than that. The church as a whole, and each particular expression of it, is addressed by God in such a way that its vocation is "called" into being. When attentive to the voice of God, a congregation discerns not only that vocation that is shared across the whole church, but also its particular calling to express that vocation in its own place and time. This is discerned and followed together by a community. Its vocation is so much more than the sum total of all the personal vocations that in fact, it ends up being the other way around. *Personal* vocation is shaped and molded in the context of a community that has clarity about *its* vocation. A Christian's personal sense of vocation is a derivative from that "one hope of our calling" (Eph. 4:4) shared with the whole church, those "called out" *(ekklesia)* into the mission of God!

Speaking this way about a congregation's missional vocation should also make it clear that we are trying to reclaim words like "vocation" and "call" for the whole church. The words have tended to be used, almost exclusively at times, for the clergy or others in special offices or roles within the church. For Protestants, the question, Are you called to the ministry? conjures up very clearly an image that includes seminary training and ordination to an office such as Minister of Word and Sacrament. Likewise, in Roman Catholic usage, the word *vocation* is used mostly to indicate those entering religious life, especially the priesthood. Both are restrictive. Not only is it true of all Christians that they are called to ministry and therefore possess vocations, but it is also true that the church itself is called and has a vocation. Discerning it brings the church nearer to the heart of God, the caller.

The stories we tell are of congregations for whom it has been important to discern their vocation. And once known, to whatever degree of clarity, it has been their intent to pursue it and fulfill it. This has set them on a path that continually asks questions of location and identity. They have given attention to:

- *where* they are, in a geographic, social, cultural context
- *when* they are, in the flow of history and change
- *who* they are, in continuity with a tradition, re-forming it in the present
- *why* they are, welcoming God's call, entering God's coming reign

(For a look at *"how* they are" in light of all this, see the other seven "patterns of faithfulness.") Following this path has required conversions of them, over and over again. But it has become the route of joy and hope for them because in their missional vocation is to be found their participation in the very life of God.

Local Responsibility — The *"Where* Are We?" Question

Holy Ghost's sense of responsibility is local, specific, geographic. If their missional assignment is clear socially and ethnically, it is because the geographic turf defines it that way. Its meeting place ("the House of the Lord"), and its residency, family by family, lie within a specific, poor, and socially rugged neighborhood, marked off by the boundaries of roads and ravines and political units. The move to that place, and thus that missionary territory, was a conscious one, prompted by the need to find a new facility. But at an important level, the church chose a facility and a neighborhood at the same time.

Transfiguration Parish, on the other hand, did not move its location 40 years ago when its present ethos began to form. Rather, the social character of the neighborhood had moved! The original immigrant population gave place to a newly arriving one, and everything was different from then on. The language went from German to Spanish. What continued were the dynamics of an immigrant population, but with a different experience of it by the new group. The economic realities meant the Puerto Rican population would have a tougher time catching hold of the ladder leading to prosperity.

In both cases, the neighborhood to which the church moved, or which moved toward the church, has had an impact on the character of the church's vocation, its sense of mission. Holy Ghost found its emphasis on "deliverance" would take on new meaning among people struggling with alcoholism, drug dealing, and family meltdown. Transfiguration was drawn to a spirituality that could sustain life together among the working poor, the street poor, and the poorest of the poor.

Eastbrook Church of Milwaukee represents another way that a sense of local responsibility came about. At its inception, the church made a deliberate choice. It was birthed in 1981 out of Elmbrook Church, a large and well-known church located in the western suburbs of Milwaukee. Its birthing represented a move not outward toward newer suburbs but in the opposite direction. A cluster of people, a number of whom lived more toward downtown, had come to share vision for a church *in* the city, and *for* the city. That early vision guided choices about the location of worship and ministry facilities, and it set the tone and character of the church. Ever since, the church's life has centered around involvement in the concerns of the city, relationships with other churches in the city, a focus of prayer upon the needs of the city, and a commitment to befriend city dwellers and welcome them to Christ.

Eastbrook's commitment to the city shows up perhaps most graphically in its clear sense of responsibility to serve city churches, regardless of denomination, by communicating personally and persistently with pastors and laypersons in order to pray for them and if possible to provide material assistance. Regularly, Eastbrook hosts worship and other activities that incorporate other churches' choirs and speakers with Eastbrook's. Two times a year, the congregation sets aside a week in which programs of ministry are set aside and the congregation gathers three times a day to pray. Each time, one of those days is focused on Milwaukee churches — their successes and their struggles. Prayer time each weekday at 6:00 a.m. throughout the year always attends to information about or from other congregations. Eastbrook sees other congregations in the region as partners, not as "them." They exist together for the city's sake.

For the West Yellowstone Presbyterian Church, the location of its responsibility comes from the character of their town. Wide swings of population between a summer season filled with tourists and service industry workers, and a winter season of year-round residents, make for an oscillating location for the church's missional vocation. The church has come to see itself as a church of and for the town part of the year and a welcoming community of worship for all for the summer visitors. They are stakeholders in both dynamics of the town's life. The character of the place has given shape to the church's vision.

Meanwhile, the IMPACT Churches of New Jersey have set upon an exciting but scary journey, taking them they know not where. Their current *raison d'etre* is to ascertain what it means for them to be the people of God today, where they are. Is it possible, they are asking, for 300-year-old Dutch Reformed congregations to develop a sense of missional vocation for a new era in vastly changed and changing surroundings? It is in quest of missional identity — and some sense of the vocation it implicates — that these seven Reformed Church in America congregations in New Jersey have embarked on a journey together. And the taproots for the missional vocation they seek are the long history of their place, their long history in it, and the place and time to which those histories have brought them and their neighbors.

What can be said most about these IMPACT churches is that they are decidedly "in process" toward a missional *identity* (who we are), missional *engagement* (what we do), missional *character* (how we do it), and missional *motivation* (why we do what we do). These four phrases best describe the purpose for which they have entered into a deliberate "process of change and transformation."

Looking back over the last five years (yes, the IMPACT congregations entered into this process only five years before our visit), one can see that their prayer, study, and intensive conversation and learning has led most of all to these results: (1) a clearer picture of the difficulty with which traditional establishment churches along the Atlantic seaboard make the change toward a community with a missional vocation, (2) a grasp of the issues that must be addressed to achieve faithful change, and (3) the renewal of focus on God's vision for the world and for the church instead of their own survival. These results have been born out of hard work and in turn bear the fruit of hope for the future! Perhaps the vocation of these churches, then — at least for now — is "discerning God's call."

Opportune Moments — The *"When* Are We?" Question

Hendrik Kraemer, a missionary leader of the middle of the twentieth century, once said, "Strictly speaking, one ought to say that the church is always in a state of crisis and that its greatest shortcoming is that it is only occasionally aware of it" (*The Christian Message in a Non-Christian World* [London: Edinburgh House, 1947, 1938c], p. 24). The Chinese character for *crisis,* we are told, is a combination of the characters for "danger" and "opportunity." Each moment presents the church with both, and that means always having to decide. What do we do now? What new opportunity and danger is facing us? What does faithfulness require in this time and place?

In a sense, what has already been said underscores the importance of time. The local particularities of a neighborhood, a city, a region, or a town are the fruit of their histories. They are what they are today, and that is different from what they were yesterday or what they will be tomorrow. To discern vocation in terms of place is also to discern it in terms of time.

But something else is important to notice in the churches we visited. That is the way in which there have been particular moments in their stories when the discernment happened. Sometimes those were sharply defined, decisive moments. Other times, it was more like the daily showers of a rainy season than a thunderstorm. Sometimes it caught their attention like a bolt of lightning. Other times it slipped in on them like the dawn of a new day or showed up more in the fading shadows of dusk — but was decisive, nonetheless.

Catalytic Moment

The arrival of the young priest, Father Bryan Karvelis, came at a time when the German-rooted life of Transfiguration Parish was at a low ebb and a fundamental re-rooting of congregational life had to take place. It was a moment when the situation demanded what a young, risk-taking priest brought by way of new vision. This was a critical moment for establishing the spirituality of Charles de Foucauld and the experiments in the forms of parish life that followed. A new direction commenced.

Not unlike that were the circumstances of Rockridge United Methodist Church in Oakland in 1988. The congregation was nearing the brink of death. Pastor David McKeithen was appointed to attempt to "revitalize" the church. Soon a team of six additional leaders came together who shared a vision. Influenced by Church of the Savior in Washington, D.C., InterVarsity Christian Fellowship (a university ministry), and memories of the importance of Wesley's class meeting structure for discipleship accountability, a new direction was forged. It was a catalytic moment.

Rockridge sees its vocation in a way that is unique among the churches we visited. Its intent is to be a community of Mission Covenant Groups, and each of those groups is expected to discern its God-given vocation. Therefore, local responsibility is multiple, and the church's "turf" is a patchwork of places and social contexts where the groups live in missional covenant. But each part of the mosaic is vivid and strong because it is rooted so deeply in the commitments and bonds of a small intentional group of disciples.

Each Mission Covenant Group at Rockridge devotes itself primarily to its respective neighborhood or social niche, and therefore each group has its own charism, its own organizing principle. One seeks to meet educational needs in the community through such means as an in-service workshop for teachers in the local school. Another is an artistic group that uses its talents in proclamation through "outdoor art," making an effort to draw disparate elements of the surrounding community together and get them talking to one another. Another group is working with people in the technology industry, and offers classes for people in the area who need to learn how to use computers. One Rockridge group builds homes for the poor in connection with Habitat for Humanity. A group made up of people from several different Mission Covenant Groups engaged in an experiment in communal housing. The latter purchased a plot of land and hired an architect to design such a place, incorporating separate apartments with shared community space that includes a kitchen and dining facility.

In the end, it is the overall vocation — and charism — of Rockridge to live "intently" with one another in missional accountability. And that bold experiment, which has not been without its difficulties, came about at a critical moment when it was possible to start down a new path.

Smoldering Vision

But a catalytic moment with the potential to focus a church's missional vocation is only one of the ways vocation becomes clear to a church. For other churches we visited, discerning vocation emerged more out of instincts that had been simmering for a long time. Somewhere beneath the surface, at times showing up above the surface, certain perspectives and practices seemed to smolder, waiting for the time when they are fanned into flame by something new in the situation or someone new in the mix. A recognition of the church's calling comes to clarity as the church makes the "obvious decision of the moment." Holy Ghost Church illustrates this pattern: the mantra "love everybody," a prophetic utterance by a Nigerian archbishop to "go to your Jerusalem," a search for an available facility in the city and not out in the megachurch-supporting suburbs, a vision to "relocate" into a community of need — a cluster of decisions, each leading to the next. In the end, clarity about its calling.

The move to establish Eastbrook Church as a church in and for the city of Milwaukee came from the instincts of a number of people. The story you get about that depends on who you ask. Some will tell you they and others at Elmbrook Church had the idea first and began meeting in their homes within the city in anticipation of becoming a church there. They talked with Elmbrook folks about allowing Marc Erickson, an M.D. and by that time a key teacher in the Elmbrook Church, to come be their pastor-preacher. If you ask Marc, it had come to be a vision of his to start a church in the city that led to the initiative. If you ask others, they might tell you that the Elmbrook pastor, Stuart Brisco, had the vision and approached Marc to encourage him to start a city church. But no matter. The diversity of stories tells us that there was general ferment in the direction of founding a church with the vocation to *be* in the city. It coalesced into what Eastbrook Church has come to be today.

As we have observed, Eastbrook's vocation is framed in terms of the "city." In one sense, that is an intentionally broad sense of the locale of its responsibility in mission. In its earlier years, it used worship and ministry facilities that were located near the University of Wisconsin (Milwaukee) campus. That particular neighborhood lent some of the character of what it meant to be a church for the city, but the church's view was always larger than a neighborhood. Its relationships and practices said it saw its vocation larger than that, but never apart from it, either. This is illustrated by what happened in the course of the church's move to new facilities in the late 1990s. Having outgrown the capacities of the prior facilities, a search was on for a new place. It was assumed this must be found within the city. One site was found, but in the end negotiations failed to establish proper zoning, so a further search was made. Finally, they came to purchase the campus of a Roman Catholic parish that had merged with another. While this was now in a new section of the city, the city focus continued. But the city focus meant that whatever immediate neighborhood surrounded their facility was an important place to which they had a calling as well. One of the early initiatives among the people of the neighborhood was a weekday youth program. One couple, who were among some of the earliest members of Eastbrook, began to establish relationships with teenagers met through the new program and then with their families. Quickly they discerned how awkward it was for them to move along the streets and among the families of the neighborhood as people who lived some distance away. They noticed a duplex for sale and decided to buy it as "investment" property (double meanings are welcomed!). That gave them a reason to be there, and made them stakeholders in the welfare of the neighborhood. The tangible rootedness of their action is what makes commitment to "the city" more than a vague generality!

The missional vocation of the West Yellowstone Presbyterian Church sort of grew on them. There was no earthshaking moment of decision or revelation. It grew out of a long history. The church had come to play a certain role for the permanent-resident town and for the tourist-season resort. It had members and officers from among both groups of residents, and that kept focus on being faithful in both directions. It was during the time before the present co-pastors arrived that this sense of mission seemed to crystallize. During the period of pastoral search, it was in their prayers that the leaders were led toward this vision of being a town-tourist church. Something was dawning on them about how God had shaped them and where that was leading.

Conscious Reflection

For other churches, missional vocation grows out of a conscious process of reflection together about God's calling. It may be stimulated by changing circumstances surrounding the church, or a sense of aimlessness within, or nagging tugs from biblical images that haunt the church with another picture of the way things ought to be.

For the IMPACT churches, it was a sense of the growing distance between their character as churches and the nature of the world around it. That led them to band together in a new way as churches living out of a common heritage and facing a common situation. They committed themselves to a collective process seeking discernment. Together they have grappled with their Reformed heritage to know themselves better. They have studied their context to get to know the kinds of people who live in it and the fundamental assumptions people in their region live by. They have explored biblical themes that call into question assumptions and practices of the past and call into being new ones. By partnering together to read the context, identify the shaping factors of the heritage, and explore new moves to make, the pastors and key leaders of the churches are framing a new question for all in the congregations to learn to engage.

For the Spring Garden Church of Willowdale, in Toronto, the key word may well be "attentiveness." Spring Garden has for many years met and worshiped in a facility tucked into a residential neighborhood of Willowdale. Their building is only a few blocks from the business district and civic center of North York, an aggressive urban development on the north side of Toronto that is now incorporated into an expanded Metro Toronto. The neighborhood of the facility and adjoining neighborhoods have experienced further change by the onset of the phenomenon of the so-called monster homes, which are large extended-family dwellings displacing the smaller bungalow homes of the area.

What has been striking about Spring Garden is how they have given increasing attention to these things. John McLaverty, after 18 years as their pastor, did extensive research into the social history by which the modern "edge city" of North York had come be a new kind of urban space. Ethnographic interviews put him and the church in touch with Asian populations now finding their home in the area. As he learned, so did the other staff and officers of the church. This contextual "reality therapy" was matched with theological exploration into the nature and witness of the church. They joined the ferment around the notion of "missional church," which led them to see themselves in new ways. Ultimately, this meant forging a fresh notion guiding the roles of staff ("mission team") and of the pastor ("mission team leader"). It meant a congregation-wide reflection of the missional nature of the church. It meant developing a clearer idea of the church's mission ("Christ in the City"). Attentiveness to organizational styles and assumptions inherited by virtue of its being a Canadian Baptist church led to fresh patterns for encouraging the missional initiatives of all the members by setting a tone of freedom and spontaneity. Paths of conscious reflection on missional character have led to a predisposition to be responsive to concerns across the city in Christ's name and in Christ's way. They have become a people able to respond nimbly and quickly to each moment's opportunity.

In Bellevue, an affluent city just east of Seattle, First Presbyterian Church has enjoyed a long history as a metropolitan area church. Like many other large, West Coast, evangelical Presbyterian churches, it has the heritage of being a church with deep roots in biblical study and knowledge, commitment to personal evangelism, and involvement in the support of global mission efforts. Its style of worship is pastorally warm with a moderately classical style of hymnody and choral expression. When members are asked what drew them to this church, over and over again the response is "the pastor" (Dick Leon) and his thoughtful and personal preaching.

Like many churches of its style and size and age, Bellevue First faces the pressure to be a "full-service church" with well-run programs to serve the interests and needs of all potential attenders and members, of all ages and backgrounds. A large and efficient staff attests to the church's commitment to respond to that. But it is evident that in the midst of that there are rumblings about the shape and direction of this 2,500-member church, motivated by questions about its proper sense of vocation. The pastor in his preaching has worked to cultivate a "missional church" perspective for the church, and he has led the elders into intentional theological reflection on that theme and others crucial to their leadership. Program staff indicate a hunger for personal relationships among the people of the church beyond their program management assignments. Work is being done to establish small groups throughout the congregation as a fabric for cultivating community and discipleship. Extensive work is being done to train the 120 deacons for their important ministries of helps. The Alpha Course is being introduced as a way that hospitality-based evangelism can be done in the congregation. A high school completion program for dropouts from the school system is hosted in the church's facility. Full-orbed training for cross-cultural ministry is provided for members who are the congregation's agents in sister-church relationships and short-term mission ventures in specific parts of the world where continuing connections are being nurtured. In all of it, the discernment and engagement is done in the midst of the tension between a provider-of-goods-and-services orientation and the church's formation as a missional community with a clear sense of vocation.

Dialogue with Tradition — The *"Who* Are We?" Question

The churches we visited are rooted in different ecclesial traditions: United Methodist, Roman Catholic, Evangelical, Baptist, Presbyterian, Pentecostal, Mennonite, and Reformed. Those differences show up. They would be recognizable to anyone knowledgeable about the traditions in which they have been formed. But that is not the whole story. For each of them, discerning their missional vocation has inevitably meant having a fresh conversation with their tradition. They have had to ask questions about what in their tradition will nourish their missional vocation and what will hinder it. They have probed their traditions to discover untapped resources. They have drawn on their tradition, recovered it, and enhanced it. And they have also differentiated themselves from it at fundamental points, critiquing it and changing it. Vocational discernment has made it clearer to them that they have a tradition and that it is important to their missional identity today. And it has made it clearer to them that their missional engagement today tests and refines and reforms that tradition as new potentials in it are discovered.

The Boulder Mennonite Church in Colorado was especially challenged by the prospect of living its tradition in a seemingly inhospitable place. The church has found Boulder to be a very secular and very wealthy place. The New Age spiritualities popular there are not Mennonite spiritualities! A community formed around a Mennonite ethic of simplicity can be something of an oddity when it is plopped down in one of the 10 wealthiest counties in the USA.

The challenge for the Boulder Church was to embody their inherited values within the social context in such a way that they are made present and accessible to others. They would have to be the kind of community that sustained each other in lifestyle choices. They would have to work out a way not to be separatist in character, an affliction that sometimes affects communities with strong countercultural convictions. They would have to be more than a community that by virtue of its tradition *stood* for peace, and be a community that *enacted and contributed* peace. That was the challenge that would lead them to weave a tight connection between a theology of reconciliation and the practice of it. So, among other things, they initiated and pioneered the Victim-Offender Reconciliation Program (VORP).

The Mennonite tradition is strong, even for those who did not grow up in it and only encountered it once they came into this congregation. But its tangible styles have had to be formed in the crucible of God's calling and their social context. Some of that happens in their small groups. Each one discerns for itself its missional focus, and while there is some ambiguity about how all the groups' efforts are connected, several things seem to stand out. The concern for reconciliation and peacemaking is a major strand in it all. Also, the dedication to "meeting human needs" is prominent. And for a number of the groups, there is special concern for what goes on on "the hill."

"The hill" is a part of the city near the university that is the site of notable social protest and conflict. On hearing about the "rainbow kids" living on the streets on the hill and the pressures from store owners and others to have them removed, one of the small groups decided to make burritos to take to the kids. They got in the habit of it and continued for three months until finally the kids were run off. On another occasion there were mounting tensions between rioting students and police on the hill, and four or five members decided to go to the hill. There they walked cautiously but decidedly among the police and the students, offering themselves as a "third presence" in the interest of peace. These are examples of ways the church has learned to deal with their peace legacy as a mandate, as their vocation.

The small mission-oriented groups of the Boulder Church are similar to those of the Rockridge Church in Oakland. But in the case of Rockridge, the precedent for that is John Wesley's "class meeting," with its system of "class leaders." The retrieval of the accountability and focused discipleship of the class meeting structure is a conscious part of Rockridge's conversation with its heritage, a heritage buried deep in Methodism but in many respects lost to contemporary practice. But with some others within the United Methodist Church, Rockridge is intent on recovering from that lost tradition. Another recent tradition, the innovative form of community in the Church of the Savior in Washington, D.C., is part of the mix as tradition sharpens tradition.

This dialogue with tradition(s) has not been painless, of course. The commitment of the leadership to focus the church around Mission Covenant Groups has not met with universal approval in the church. The difficulty of winding up with two tiers of membership — the group-participating members and the worship-attending members — has yet to be resolved in practice. But even the difficulty constitutes a dialogue with numerous renewal traditions in the history of the Christian church that have come up against similar problems.

As a Roman Catholic parish, certain features of organization and liturgical practice at Transfiguration are fixed. The parish does not have, nor would it want to have, the measure of local choice that even congregations within mainline Protestant denominations have, let alone the local autonomy of churches in a Baptist polity or independent churches. And yet, within the tradition there are traditions that provide possibilities for innovative approaches to community, leadership, and liturgy. Particularly, the spirituality of Charles de Foucauld and the patterns of the Base Ecclesial Communities of Latin America are overlays on the fixed structures that have become an inherent part of the missional fabric of the congregation.

The effort at Transfiguration has been to generate a kind of discipleship that combines aspects of the traditional Catholic parish with what it means to be an intentional community. This touches the organizational structure of the parish. The focus on intentional community has been most apparent in the work to sustain the strong network of fraternities — small Christian communities within the parish that meet in homes throughout the area. The responsibles who lead them, by their weekly meditation, worship, discernment, and planning together on Saturday mornings, have become the center of decision making for the parish. The responsibles have come to function as the parish council.

The celebration of the mass contains a homily that has been influenced by the ways the fraternities engaged the same lectionary texts during the preceding week. It is the intention of Father Bryan to use the mass to relate Christ to the contemporary situation of the congregation. He sees it as a liturgical framework for contextual communication, so liturgy is adapted to the lives of the people. The sanctuary itself reflects the core commitments. The chancel has been stripped of the ornate, and in its place are bare symbols appropriate to the spirituality the community is called to follow: to be present with Christ in the Eucharist, and present with the poorest of the poor.

An interesting mixture of traditions converges in what Holy Ghost Church is today. A visit to their annual Founders Day celebration helps to sort out the various strands. Worship pastor Val McCune is the team historian, and she provides a historical map, with pictures and notations to highlight the people who embodied the various traditions from which they have grown. This includes leaders in the Missionary Baptist and National Baptist traditions who first formed the church in the 1940s and led it through its early years. It includes early founding leaders of what came to be called Pentecostalism, a stream that has come into the life of Holy Ghost in recent decades (marked by the addition of "Full Gospel" to the church's name). It includes American and African leaders in the International Communion of Charismatic Churches with which the church is associated. Even beyond what makes it onto the formal map, the church's character is shaped by traditions such as the ministry approach of John Perkins and the Voice of Calvary and the liturgical renewal influences of Robert Webber.

Along with the shaping influence of all these traditions comes a necessary dialogue at critical points. In particular, the church sees itself at odds with choices made by many companions within African-American Pentecostal and Baptist circles who have seemed to exchange the message of deliverance and holiness for one of health and wealth. The Nigerian connection places the church in relationship with churches like the one there that recently opened a 50,000-seat sanctuary and had 40,000 in worship on the first Sunday! The natural instinct toward self-questioning (Why isn't this happening here?) and self-doubt (Why isn't God blessing us that way?) sets afoot another kind of dialogue. It forces the church to know its own environment better and to see the difference between the cultures of America and Nigeria at the present moment. It brings to sharper relief the differences in spiritual hunger, fundamental worldview, and religious moods. The post-Christian character of American sensibilities and the religious consumerism of an individualistic society become new factors that confirm the church's commitment to refuse to pitch the church to what would draw the crowds in today's Detroit.

The city location and focus of Eastbrook's life has meant it has become different from its parent Elmbrook Church. But the difference is not total. The theological heritage and evangelical cast of the church's life and style have roots there that remain evident. Identifying the threads of traditions held and valued within the congregation is evident at two special points. Along the way, Pastor Marc Erickson has prepared extensive notes on theological themes important to the leadership of the church, showing their continuities with a full range of ecclesial traditions, including not only evangelical and Protestant but Roman Catholic and Eastern Orthodox traditions. He attempts to show the whole family tree and the church's relation to it. The effort is certainly part of the church's impulse to value and be in partnership with churches of all sorts in the city and not to conceive of itself as an isolated, self-sufficient church. Also, the worship leadership, during the early years of the church, gave serious attention to the development of a theology of worship. The fruit of that work still remains the touchstone, and the theology that orients worship shows the marks of dialogue with a number of traditions, many of which have come into this "independent, community church" in the memories and practices of members whose prior church experience was in congregations of other denominations, including mainline Protestant churches and the Roman Catholic Church.

For some of the churches we visited, the dialogue with tradition is not so much with what we would normally understand to be the distinctiveness of their particular denominational traditions, theological or liturgical. Rather, it is with the accumulated patterns of "being an organization" that have shaped the way things are done in North American churches in general. This seems to be the case with Spring Garden, where there is a certain caution or distance from the accepted ways of operating assumed within the Canadian Baptist system of which it is a part. The issue is, "How are we supposed to be the church?" and the established answers to that question are challenged by Spring Garden's pursuit of a lifestyle that plays out a missional understanding of the church and the present context in which the church lives.

In similar fashion, the Reformed churches of the IMPACT group and the Presbyterian churches in West Yellowstone and Bellevue dialogue not only with their Reformed heritage but with the more recent experience of Reformed and other mainline denominations that has to do with organizational form. Many scholars have demonstrated that fundamental operating assumptions of the twentieth-century church — denominationally and congregationally — have formed under the shaping influence of American corporate styles. (See for example Milton J. Coalter, John M. Mulder, and Louis B. Weeks, eds., *The Organizational Revolution,* Vol. 6 in *The Presbyterian Experience* [Louisville: Westminster/John Knox, 1991]). These churches wrestle, sometimes more consciously and sometimes less, with the way values such as economy of scale, efficiency, rational order and control, division of labor, and specialization have left us with a kind of church that is more like a "vendor of religious services and goods" than a "body of people sent on a mission." (See *Missional Church,* pp. 83ff.) The dialogue is at points more emphatically an engagement with American pragmatic traditions than it is with a particular ecclesial and theological tradition.

Continuous Cultivation — The *"Why* Are We?" Question

A congregation's sense that it has a missional vocation, and its idea of what that vocation is, comes about out of the crucible of struggle. The circumstances of the church's context, the resources (and liabilities) of the church's tradition, and the voice of God in the biblical word are all a part of the mix. Discernment emerges in multiple ways, but always these are the crucial factors.

But discernment and vocation are not one-time matters. Discerning is a constant challenge, as is following. Yesterday's discernments are met by today's new questions and visions. So it is important to notice in the churches we visited how they cultivate and nourish their sense of missional vocation in continuing ways.

When a church like Holy Ghost takes up residence in a neighborhood — their personal residence as well as the place where their gatherings reside — the continuous cultivation comes pretty naturally. Their vocation is the neighborhood, and they're always there! They're on the streets, in the homes, and along the alleyways. They are *present* to the neighborhood, and they're a part of the neighborhood. So the vocation stays vivid.

In addition, the strong bonds among the group of pastors and elders and the synergy of their various ministries continue to nurture vision at the center. If an aspect of that fades, once noticed it is quickly rebuilt, because core leadership people are around. Their lives intertwine. Newer leadership is consciously drawn into the central dynamic that sets the tone for the whole.

Spring Garden has the habit of praying, and on periodic occasions they do that together on a Saturday morning "prayer walk." Sometimes as many as 100 of them will gather, and in smaller clusters walk the streets of the urban strip a few blocks away, or the neighborhood bungalows, or the newer monster homes, praying as they go. They pray for shopkeepers, for civic officials, for corporations, for older residents on fixed income, for young families starting out, for wealthy new Asian immigrants, for whomever comes to their attention as they walk and watch and listen. This habit keeps them in touch with what their study has identified. But it keeps it personal. It keeps it up to date. It keeps it vivid, fixing the direction of their vocation.

In Spring Garden, missional team leader John McLaverty plays the important role of continuing to focus the energy of the congregation. But he doesn't do that by setting the agenda for them. He creates a climate where that can happen. He practices at the center the values placed on the readiness to respond with spontaneity and grace.

Eastbrook Church had from the beginning a clear direction. They were to be a church of, and in, and for the city. Particular expressions of that have always had to be worked out. But clarity about what guides the choices has been maintained. To the present time, the "city-ness" of their vocation is a topic that calls forth the conversation about what God wants them to do.

The vision is maintained because the central values it entails are over and over again articulated and demonstrated and rehearsed. The community practices what it means to be a church for the city. They perform that central conviction at every opportunity.

As might be expected, Pastor Marc plays a large role in keeping the core story alive and tangible. For example, the unity with other churches which is so large a part of how Eastbrook sees itself as a church for the city is expressed in numerous ways in Marc's comments, illustrations, communications, attitudes and actions. There is no mistaking how much of a core value this is for him as well as the church. But Marc is not alone. Worship leadership, for example, sets the tone from the very beginning in the worship gatherings. They serve notice: "We are in partnership with Christ's other churches in the city and we do not seek or encourage people to leave those churches to join us here."

In a more direct and deliberate way, the Rockridge Church and the Boulder Church maintain continuous attention on the matter of discerning missional vocation by expecting that in each of the small groups. That of course requires nurturing and accountability, but their groups function at high levels in the practice of discernment.

The Boulder Church takes that one step farther. In addition to what the groups do regarding their own particular mission focus, the whole congregation is gathered in retreat once a year for what is called "mapmaking," an exercise of ministry discernment. They ask, "What is our ministry? Who are we? What are we about?" The purpose is to keep the central mission vision of the congregation lively and refreshed, and to ensure that the vision is pressed into the fabric of all the activities of the church.

In a similar fashion, Transfiguration has built into its rhythm of life occasions for continuing to ask the discernment questions. In one way, this is a weekly routine. The fraternities read the lectionary texts and ask how this informs their vocation and shapes them for it. The responsibles meet weekly with each other and Father Bryan, and together they seek to discern the voice of the Spirit through the Scriptures and through their contemplation of Christ in the Eucharist. But then, every six months the responsibles go on retreat together for an extended time. Their primary purpose is to discern what the congregation needs to hear during the next half year. It is an exercise in anticipating what God wants to say to them next and how that will lead them in their vocation. Out of this discernment, the agenda for the small fraternities is set.

Vocation and Charism

In the previous chapter, we gave basic descriptions of the churches we visited. In those, we tried to show what we had observed in each to be its "charism," its special gift. We return to that notion now in order to make some connections we think are important and may be useful to churches reading this book.

We have suggested that it is appropriate to use the term *vocation* for a congregation's calling as well as for an individual's calling. The term *charism* is an English rendering of the New Testament Greek word for "gift," and it has to do with the gifts the Holy Spirit gives to Christian believers. The "gifts" are practices and abilities specially given to each to be used for the common good of the Christian community, and they are the means for ministering the grace of Christ to one another. And at least once in the New Testament, the word *gifts* is used in reference to those special persons given to the community for equipping all for the work of ministry (Eph. 4:10-11). Roman Catholics use the term *charism* to speak about these gifts. Protestants tend to use the language of "spiritual gifts."

Here we are daring to suggest that just as the term *vocation* can be used of congregations, so can *charism*. There is precedent for this in Roman Catholic usage, as when a religious order or community is said to have a particular charism, that is, a special gift which they offer to the whole Christian community. It is tied closely to the vocation of such a community, something they have especially been called to do on behalf of the whole church. It is in that sense that we have used the word *charism* in reference to the churches we have visited. Their charism is that unique trait, that particular feature of the congregation's life and contribution that comes from the exercise of the vocation they have discerned to be theirs.

To illustrate: One of the authors of this book was pastor of the Covenant Presbyterian Church of Biloxi, Mississippi, in the 1970s. That fairly new and small congregation found itself, little by little, ministering in a range of ways among children and teenagers. That was not only because of the high proportion of teenagers in the families of the church. There were other factors. For one thing, the teenagers of the church's families brought in many of their peers, and that swelled the youth group. But also, a number of families in the church, somewhat independently of each other at first, began to volunteer at the local youth court. That involved things like extended care for infants awaiting the outcome of custody matters, weekend care for delinquent teenagers awaiting the adjudication of their cases, or big brother/big sister relationships with troubled kids. At points it involved formal adoption into one of the families of the church. It also involved points of advocacy for children within the community. But there had never been a formal decision that children and youth were the church's missional calling, or that the church thought it had that spiritual gift. It simply emerged as a characteristic response of the church to what seemed to be important to God. What emerged was something like the charism of that church.

What we have identified to be the charism of each of these churches we visited is intimately linked to the vocation they have discerned and followed. As is the case with an individual's spiritual gifts, or charisms, a congregation's recognition of its charism derives from the faithful fulfillment of its vocation. To be called to a particular vocation does not necessarily mean that God sends us to do what we feel we are good at, what we are gifted for, or what we would enjoy doing. Biblical accounts of callings illustrate that the more normal pattern is that callings tend to involve the same forms of suffering and sacrifice that Jesus' calling did. The gift of the Spirit to fulfill the calling comes in the course of the faithful response. It becomes evident only over time what that gift, that charism, has been. Once evident, its presence in the pulse of a congregation's life is a gift to the whole church toward the fulfillment of its missional nature. And in fact, it is a gift from God to the world that is coming to know Christ because this charism has come to expression in this congregation that takes its vocation seriously.

> The calling of the church to be missional — to be a sent community — leads the church to step beyond the given cultural forms that carry dubious assumptions about what the church is, what its public role should be, and what its voice should sound like. Testing and revising our assumptions and practices against a vision of the reign of God promises the deep renewal of the missional soul of the church that we need. By daily receiving and entering the reign of God, through corporate praying for its coming, and longing for its appearance, and in public living under its mantle, this missional character of the church will be nourished and revived. (*Missional Church,* p. 109)

Pattern 2

Biblical Formation and Discipleship

DARRELL L. GUDER

"We have the same spirit of faith that is in accordance with scripture. . . . Even though our outer nature is wasting away, our inner nature is being renewed day by day."

(2 Cor. 4:13, 16)

Pattern: The missional church is a community where all members are learning what it means to be disciples of Jesus. The Bible has a continuing, converting, formative role in the church's life.

Well into their process, the IMPACT congregations realized the centrality of biblical formation to the process of missional change. "We're involved in lots of theological reading and study — it's now an ongoing thing in this congregation." "An increased number of persons have become willing to participate in Bible study. . . . There is definitely more of a servant attitude as a result of this study. There's a change in perception about what we're after as a church. This actually could be quite a major shift. People are looking at church in a different way."

Becoming a missional congregation can be described as a process of biblical formation and discipling. This was an assumption that we took with us into the congregations we examined. We conjectured that (in the words of our initial criteria for the missional congregation) "biblical formation and discipling [would be] essential for members," and that "the missional church is a community where all members [would be] involved in learning to become disciples of Jesus." If that had not been a criterion going in, it would have surfaced immediately. In every congregation, the commitment to biblical formation, focusing in some way on discipleship as the norm for Christian life and practice, was observable. Yet, here again we had to learn that the reality is much more complex and even ambiguous than any neatly formulated criterion could foresee. What does it really mean to live "in accordance with scripture" and to experience the daily renewal of our inner natures which, in our view, is what discipleship is all about?

Not All Bible Study Is Missional Formation

It may seem more than obvious that the Bible should stand at the center of the missional church. Virtually every Christian tradition affirms the centrality of Scripture to the Christian church. In theory at least, the sermon preached every Sunday is a proclamation of the biblical word. Certainly all of the congregations under review would make such affirmations and expect such preaching from their ministers.

There is a problem, however. It is possible to be biblically centered, to expect and to experience biblical preaching, and not to be a church that acknowledges, much less practices, its missional calling. This is the crisis and the dilemma of much of the Western church. It is possible to study the Scriptures in such a way that its central emphasis upon formation for mission is missed. It is possible to hear the gospel primarily in terms of what God's grace does for me, or for you. It is possible to take the Bible seriously, persuaded that it is primarily about one's personal salvation. It is possible to preach the Bible in such a way that the needs of persons are met but the formation of the whole community for its witness in the world is not emphasized. It is, in short, possible to be Bible-centered and not wholeheartedly missional.

Dallas Willard has said that our churches are full of converts who do not intend to become disciples. Another way to put it would be this: Our churches are full of people who are there to receive the benefits of grace without knowing that they are receiving such blessings "in order to be a blessing." In such congregations, mission tends to be one of many programs done by the community, rather than to define the very purpose and character of the community. Mission sermons are preached now and again in order to mobilize action or resources for a particular outreach. People know that mission is a theme of the Bible, and they expect to hear about it now and again. But discipling is rarely focused on mission. It is primarily understood, where it is talked about, as a process of personal spiritual growth.

The Biblical Shape of Missional Formation

The first Christian communities shared the conviction that they existed for Christ's mission. They were the result of the apostolic mission, and their purpose was to continue that mission. They understood that they were to live their life together "worthy of the calling to which they had been called" (see 1 Thess. 2:12; Phil. 1:27; Eph. 4:1). Their calling was to "be my witnesses" (Acts 1:8). To use a contemporary expression, they understood themselves to be "missionary by their very nature."

How do such missional communities happen? What forms them? Our discussion of the patterns of missional congregations will make plain that there are many dimensions to the formation of such churches. But the fundamental answer we anticipated is what we found: biblical discipling is crucial. The missional transformation of a congregation is directly related to the priority assigned to the Bible and to the way in which the Bible shapes that community.

The Gospels describe how Jesus called together his disciples and intensively trained them for the mission that would follow. Their discipline was a "going to school with Jesus" — and their graduation was the call to be apostles. Jesus' disciples became his "sent-out ones," his witnessing people, empowered by the Holy Spirit. The Twelve whom Jesus called became the founding generation of the church. As they lived with Jesus, learned his message, watched his actions, they were being molded by him to become salt, leaven, and light in the world. His ministry reached its climax at the cross and Easter. With the gift of the Holy Spirit at Pentecost, it now became the ministry of the community initiated by the Twelve. Every community that follows after them and is built upon their foundation is, in the same way, called together by Jesus and is being formed by him for his mission. The fraternities in Transfiguration Parish express perhaps mostly concretely this commitment to formation by Jesus through following him in disciplined grappling with the biblical message. But, as we shall see, that formation is at the heart of every congregation under review.

With this pattern we are addressing the most ancient and essential characteristic of the church: Jesus personally formed the first generation of Christians for his mission. After that, their testimony became the tool for continuing formation. At the beginning it was their oral testimony, the message they passed on as the first missionaries. We see this ministry in the speeches in Acts and in the accounts of the early missionary spread of the church. With time, this oral proclamation became written testimony, in the form of letters and distinctive stories called Gospels. They were gradually drawn together in the collection of writings that became the Bible. The purpose of this "Word of God written" was and is the continuing formation of the missional church. Every Christian is called to be a follower of Jesus whom he is making into a "fisher of people." The life of the New Testament churches was centered around their missional vocation and their formation to practice it. This is what discipling was all about. This formation happens as the biblical word works powerfully within the community.

What we observe in missional congregations is a shared sense of calling to follow Jesus, and a growing desire to be formed by the Bible for his service. Although it happens in many ways, the Bible is normative for the life of such churches. Listening to and responding to the Bible is the way Christians learn "how to follow Jesus, the carpenter of Nazareth," as the lay fraternities at Transfiguration put it — and in their case, this happens by following in "the footsteps of Brother Charles de Foucauld." However the question is posed, the Bible must continue to confront, to convert, and to transform the community for faithful witness. It is the instrument God's Spirit uses to bring about renewal: "our inner nature is being renewed day by day."

Moving toward Biblical Formation: Tension and Change

Most scholars would agree that there is an essential linkage between missionary vocation and biblical formation, between apostolate and discipling. Yet, it should be no surprise that we discovered a range of attitudes and reactions among the reviewed congregations when we tried to understand how they understood their mission, and how biblical discipling related to it. For congregations of mainline traditions there can be distinctive problems in recognizing the urgency and radical character of biblical formation for mission. Such churches look back upon centuries of tradition, creeds, confessions, theology, and even missionary activity. There is an understandable sense that "we know what it's all about." People form and join such churches, often, in order to continue the religious life they have been accustomed to, to guarantee the maintenance of the Christian traditions they have inherited.

This is often a real struggle for the pastoral and lay leadership of a congregation. They often recognize the changed situation of our North American context. They see that our culture has become a mission field. They deeply desire to lead their communities into a transformed awareness of their own missionary calling. In their preaching and teaching, these themes are becoming central. But there is great resistance to the missional transformation of the church, particularly among the self-confident heirs of mainline traditions. To hear the well-known biblical message in this new way (which is really a very ancient way of hearing it!) is even threatening to Christian communities whose vision is "to keep on keeping on."

The problem lies deeply embedded within the North American culture that has designated the church and its life part of the private and individual sector. The church is a "free-time activity." It functions as a purveyor of programs designed to "meet the needs" of its members. Its role in the life of its members is always controlled by their "opting to participate." In this context, it is difficult to establish biblical formation and missional discipleship as a binding commitment and recognized priority. Biblical formation as an option creates a profound tension. The expectation that missional discipleship "will be fun, easy, entertaining, and will meet my needs" contributes to this tension.

To be sure, where this kind of transforming biblical formation begins to happen, then there is change, although not without resistance. One pastor from the IMPACT churches reports, regarding the critically important role of Bible study in their process: "As a result of Bible study there has been movement among people away from giving definitive answers to asking and dwelling in the questions, such as, 'What does God really want of us as a church?'" To get to that question has been a costly process in this cluster of congregations. We frequently found evidences of this tension, an indication that missional ferment is happening.

At Bellevue Presbyterian, the pastoral leaders and many of the lay leaders are struggling with this tension. A Bible study participant reported, "The reason for our growth is the Bible-based nature of this church. The lordship of Jesus Christ and the truth of the Scriptures — this emphasis has been descriptive of all the senior pastors here." The pastoral leadership is encouraged that members see this priority so clearly, but they also recognize that there is a tendency to define both "lordship" and "scriptural truth" in individualistic ways. So the senior pastor is working both in the pulpit and with his leaders to grapple with the missionary vocation of the church. They candidly admit that many are listening selectively. They are responding to strong biblical preaching, but they want to hear a message about "what the gospel does for you," and they want to have their spiritual needs met. Discipling is an option that is offered, and it is taken seriously by many. It is evoked persistently, but the emphasis is gentle and invitational, and it usually centers around getting involved in one of the many ministries of the church. One can remain anonymous in the church, come and go as one pleases, hearing and deriving genuine benefit from the clear gospel message of grace. Many, however, can do that and filter out the missional calling which is at the core of the gospel. After all, we have centuries behind us in which we have done precisely that.

The size of the congregation is not the telling factor in this process of selective hearing. In the West Yellowstone congregation, which is growing dynamically and clearly attracting people into the community, there is an intentional discipling process which bonds the pastor and the lay leaders (the session). They want to see this commitment spread throughout the congregation, and there are encouraging signs that it is happening, but there are also many who come for "what they can get out of it." It is hard to communicate the missionary calling of the church to people who are persuaded that they already know what the gospel is about!

This tension is an issue for the congregations involved in the IMPACT project. They are old, established congregations with a long and honorable tradition. Their members often make it clear that they come to their churches with the expectation that the ministry they experience will improve them rather than change them. The problem of the convert who does not want to become a disciple is, in many ways, the motivation for the entire project. Raising this question has evoked a range of responses, and some of them have been very resistant. Many Christians who would certainly attest that they are serious about their faith are put off by the biblical challenge to become a truly missional church. When some respond and begin to get involved in biblical formation, a tension arises between those who are committed to scriptural discipleship and those who choose not to be. Gradually there is response among some, an opening up to the converting claims of the missionary gospel. But there is also rejection; some people leave, looking for another church which will better "meet their needs." Because these congregations have persisted in spite of resistance, they can now report that "the Bible has been essential to our framing of vision. The broad-based congregational study and exploration of the biblical calling have helped our church to overcome inertia, the problem of people sitting on the sidelines, simply watching. We haven't arrived, but we've started; we're moving."

This tension is also experienced at Rockridge and is a constant struggle. The core congregation, which went through the process of fundamental reorientation resulting in the missional commitments of the church, did not and could not bring everyone with them. There were resisters. There were those who wanted to be members of "their" church who rejected the intentional commitments and disciplines of the Mission Covenant Groups. Since these commitments have become definitive for a significant segment of the congregation, the challenge is now to work patiently and compassionately with the internal controversy and resistance. This is not easy.

In a congregation not so shaped by the mainline traditions, such as Eastbrook, this tension also exists. The opportunity for discipleship is emphasized, but it is optional and voluntary. Not everyone who is part of the congregation chooses to engage in the available structures. The decision to engage in the kinship groups symbolizes a step towards more intentional commitment. But the umbrella of the congregation is large enough to shelter those who decide to do so, and those who choose not to, at least not yet. For everyone, however, the missional challenge of the gospel is the central theme of public preaching and teaching, as is the case in all of the congregations we are discussing.

There appears to be less of this tension in the Holy Ghost congregation. There the entire environment sends a clear message, underlined in every prayer, exhortation, and message: this is a community whose members are "living into becoming a holy people." If one is not interested, it is unlikely that one would remain long. The congregation is working intentionally to become an equipping center in which discipling for mission is happening. They report that, in fact, people do leave because they are not open to this challenge to intentional discipleship.

Similarly, at Spring Garden Church, there is an overarching sense that one will not be comfortable unless one is open to becoming an activist, nourished and shaped by biblical proclamation. The assumed norm of the congregation is discipleship. It is not debatable, nor is it even discussed as such, but rather it is taken for granted. The people talk about their church as a place that provides safety, mutual care, and a willingness to shoulder large and difficult tasks. Drawn to this congregation are people who have great needs, and as they receive care, they are expected to become care providers for others. To experience mission leads to becoming part of mission.

A congregation in the Mennonite tradition, such as the Boulder Church, is defined from the outset by the distinctive commitments of the Anabaptist movement. To identify with the church and its disciplines is to signal a certain intentionality about shared mission. There are other, more comfortable, and less challenging Christian churches to attend if one does not want that kind of challenge. In this relatively small congregation, the norm is a shared commitment to move together toward discipleship, although they are modest in their claims about how far they have gotten. They will talk about the way that the community, in its small groups, worked with members whose marriage was in trouble, helping them to save it. They remember a medical doctor whose decision to invest in a very large home led to a conversation that resulted in her opting for a smaller one.

How Do Biblical Formation and Discipleship Happen?

It might sound as though the issue of biblical discipling and missionary calling is really another version of the old struggle between believers' churches and the inclusive churches of the dominant Western traditions. There are parallels. But it is too easy an equation. What Western churches have in common is a tendency to reduce the gospel to the individual and to understand the congregation as the community of the saved. They often define that salvation more or less rigorously. But the crucial issue of missional vocation can be as challenging for a believers' church as it is for a more diverse and inclusive church.

One can look at the entire spectrum of megachurches in North America and find a market-oriented understanding of the gospel: meeting needs, providing support, affirming individual salvation, and engaging in missions as one program among many. Neither size, nor success, nor vitality by any number of measurements is necessarily a guarantor that a congregation is confronting and responding to missional vocation.

As we have said, the emphasis upon the Bible in preaching and teaching does not mean that the biblical formation of a missional church is actually happening. What we perceive in a range of variations is a process of fermentation and leavening in congregations. We see groups in congregations, sometime the "core congregation," responding to the missional calling, and seeking to work out this calling responsibly within their own community and beyond. In another study, we might examine newly founded congregations whose formation was guided by the missional patterns we have identified. Our hunch is that we would find tensions similar to the ones we have seen in our cluster of churches. People come into churches already shaped by their background as heirs of Christendom. They come to new churches expecting them to continue and to maintain what has been. The challenge all along the line is one of conversion!

The reality, which confronts us everywhere in the North American context, is vividly demonstrated at Transfiguration Parish. Thousands of people live in and identify with this Roman Catholic parish; they demonstrate all the aspects of Christendom mentality we expect. However, some 300 of them are engaged in fraternities and have made together the commitment to live Christ's life in their community. The fraternal life is a calling, an option, to which the larger congregation is constantly invited as they regularly do their religious duty and come to mass. How this is happening in the congregations under review is the real issue. It is clear that the summons to missionary vocation and to the engagement with the Bible as missional formation is a *transforma-tion*, that is, a formation that moves a community to a place where it has not been. We do see in these congregations instructive and encouraging demonstrations of such transformation happening. That is what merits our attention.

In many of the congregations under review, biblical formation takes place in small groups, often with a high level of discipline and commitment. In Transfiguration Parish, the lectionary texts of Sunday worship shape much that happens during the week, especially in the fraternities. The common expectation is that the Bible will speak and transform the life and actions of this community. The fraternities meet to study the readings for the coming Sunday and to examine how the Bible guides their living and decision making. They have discovered again and again that the biblical word has directed them to concrete actions with regard to money, property, sharing resources, and reaching out into the need of their neighborhood.

The members of Holy Ghost Church assume that the Bible will shape what they believe and guide them to see what their faith must mean. There is a Bible college in place, with a set curriculum and standards, focusing on the faith and life of disciples. Elders are expected to complete this program: it is the leadership training school of the congregation.

Bible discipleship groups are described as "life changing" by members of Spring Garden Church. Membership formation begins with the well-known Alpha program, which is having a profound evangelistic impact at Spring Garden as it is in other churches across the world. But that introduction to biblical formation is followed by a strong emphasis on biblical preaching and personal biblical study in groups. Biblical learning is the basic curriculum of children's and youth work — the congregation does not rely on formal educational curricula.

In the churches of the IMPACT project, the reorientation to biblical formation has had a revolutionizing effect, in spite of the tensions it has evoked. "Study around biblical images of the church has been a foundation for our ability to work together. Without it, we surely would have gotten off again on the wrong foot, discouraged about our church, sunk in its problems and many deficiencies, becoming defensive toward each other. The Scriptures lifted our sights by offering a vision of what we are to be and what our church could become." These congregations are consciously trying to make the New Testament church their model and goal. As a result, all of their committees precede their business with Bible study, constantly asking how to be a more faithful church. They expect the biblical word to guide them in this growth process. The leadership of the cluster devotes a great deal of time to Bible study and prayer, and they have found that this concretely shapes their decisions about mission. Such discipline is a new thing in old congregations, which like many North American churches have relied upon their pastors to be the "Bible experts" on their behalf. But they have found that this biblical discipline is exciting and challenging, and that it is changing how they think and act. It has become, in their view, critical to their renewal. The encounter with the biblical word as missional formation has helped them come to terms with their traditions, and to risk moving out of old ruts. In the Rockaway Church, 75 percent of the congregation participated in a study on the Beatitudes, asking how Jesus' instruction intended to shape their church for its witness.

The congregations under review find themselves at various places on a spectrum of biblical discipline. In Bellevue, there is a vast range of educational opportunities with many forms of Bible study. The preaching ministry is strongly biblical, rooted in the conviction of biblical authority. The sheer size of such a congregation means that the levels of commitment to biblical discipline vary broadly. It also means that a great deal is happening in small groups that is largely unknown to the pastoral leadership. The challenge in such a church is to find ways to center the entire congregation around its biblical vocation.

Hearing the Bible Missionally

One way to assess the way in which biblical formation is happening in a congregation is to examine how the Bible is read and heard. Our engagement with the Bible is always defined by the questions we bring to it. As we have stressed already, even where the Bible is taken seriously, the temptation is great to approach the Bible with the question, What can I get out of this? Such an approach reflects the way our particular mission field functions: we are a self-centered society. We describe ourselves as individualistic and self-indulgent. We are easily tempted to use Scripture for our own purposes.

Where missional renewal is happening, different kinds of questions are brought to the Bible. Congregations are open to being challenged, to looking hard at their deeply ingrained attitudes and expectations. The missional approach asks, How does God's Word call, shape, transform, and send me . . . and us? Coupled with this openness is the awareness that biblical formation must mean change, and often conversion. Christian communities may discover that their discipling will require repentance and that their way of being church will have to change.

Such communities assume that no one enters the church automatically knowing how things are done in the reign of God. They recognize that our society conditions us to rewrite and adapt the biblical message to make it more palatable for us. They are discovering how important it is to be critical of the traditions we inherit because often they have fostered a dilution of biblical authority in the church.

This expectation has taken intentional shape in Transfiguration Parish. The fraternities practice the "review of life," a biblically informed exercise in which they hear the Scriptures as a challenge to the way they are leading their lives. This process has been in place for 40 years. They now look back upon significant discoveries and transformations in the lives of individuals and the congregation. Members have been led to change their professions, to relocate so that they could minister in the community more effectively, to drop practices that were unfaithful (gambling, for example), and to take on the concerns of undocumented immigrants.

Similar changes have taken place among the members of Holy Ghost Church. There, the preaching and teaching ministry emphasizes the biblical difference between holy living and the normal life of our society. The consequence is the expectation that God will heal and deliver people from addictions and destructive patterns of living. As a further consequence, people have moved into neighborhood houses near the church, believing that God has called them to a particular mission in that place. That mission entails living with the people to whom they are called and whom they serve.

The move of Rockridge United Methodist towards intentional community with covenants and disciplines was a result of biblical formation. The consensus that has shaped their community was a call to be an alternative community. As they continue to struggle with the actual shape of that calling, they expect the Bible to guide them, especially in the Mission Covenant Groups. Like every community seeking to be faithful to the biblical calling, they also grapple with the challenge of discernment. How does one, in fact, hear and understand God's formative word, especially when we are so conditioned to determine in advance what the Bible is supposed to say?

The participants in the IMPACT project in New Jersey have discovered that serious Bible study reveals how far our Western church traditions have moved from the New Testament church. Their study has widened the gap between the biblical vision and their experienced reality. It has made them more dissatisfied with the way things are, but it has also given them some tools for analyzing the situation. They are discovering biblical ways of asking questions, biblical challenges to long-held assumptions, and, gradually, biblical resources for change. In their current passage, the primary impact of the biblical challenge is to create a sense of a gap, a disconnect with the status quo — and a desire to move beyond it.

In their approach to scriptural formation, the leaders and members of Spring Garden Church expect to be challenged and unsettled. The Bible is expounded as a risky, provocative mandate, calling into question their comfort and complacency. A particular emphasis of this biblical exposition has been the emphasis upon "compassionate entrepreneurship," leading various individuals and groups to respond to the challenge by initiating a diversity of ministry projects. There have been some bold experiments, and they are willing to admit that some of them have not shown much sign of biblical formation.

Modest and Yet Hopeful Expectations

The questions one asks will define the answers one gets. We approached this spectrum of congregations with the assumption that the missional church is a community where all members are involved in learning to become disciples of Jesus. We expected that this would mean that the identity of the disciple would be held by all, and that growth in discipleship would be expected by all. In our actual encounters with these churches, we became more modest with regard to the "all." We recognized that missional transformation is a complex process. Not everyone is in the same place at the same time. But we also recognized that this was precisely the case in the New Testament churches!

Much of what we expected to find was confirmed. Congregations that are becoming missional do show some important convictions that are instructive. They know that people do not automatically know how the reign of God works. Citizenship in the reign of God is learned. They are grappling with the fact that this learning involves the behaviors and processes that witness to the way of Jesus. They are opening themselves to his formation of them for his ministry: the demonstration of God's reign breaking in. Although expressed in different ways, they are candid about the fact that they can no longer rely on "how we've always done things around here." It is not enough to say that "this is how we Baptists or Lutherans or Presbyterians or Methodists or Mennonites or Catholics have always done it." They are developing, sometimes painfully, skills in self-analysis and self-criticism, which move them close to what the Bible calls repentance. They are aware that change is hard, often painful, but unavoidable if Jesus is the one who is forming them. Their conviction is becoming more and more articulate that their formation as witnesses to God's reign is the reality which defines them.

This is seen most importantly in their relationship to biblical discipling and formation. They are reading the Bible together to learn what they can learn nowhere else: God's good and gracious intent for all creation, the good and mysterious news of salvation, their common calling. In diverse ways they are coming to two interlocking convictions: we must know the Scriptures, and we must desire to be obedient to the formative word revealed in Scriptures. Thus the biblical process more and more pervades the life of the community. This is often linked with the candid confession that they had tended to limit the power and scope of the scriptural word. Now, they are learning to risk hearing it and doing it, knowing that it might mean serious change.

These processes are by no means complete or perfect. There is debate, argument, even resistance. But biblical formation and discipling are happening. Ministers are discovering in exciting ways their distinctive vocation to be the biblical "equippers of the saints for the work of ministry" (Eph. 4:12). The missional transformation we observe happening cannot be planned, manipulated, or scheduled. But it is clear that it has to do with the congregation's growing clarity about who it is and what it is for, and its expanding engagement with the Bible as God's instrument for its missional formation. Missional churches, like their mother church in Acts, are made up of followers of the Way, who is Jesus Christ. This is a pilgrimage, a voyage, a journey, and not an arrival. Or, to use another biblical image, there is growth, maturing, a lengthening and deepening obedience, linked with ever more confident hope that God will complete the good work that he has begun among his people.

> The church is not simply a gathering of well-meaning individuals who have entered into a social contract to meet their privately defined self-interests. It is, instead, an intentional and disciplined community witnessing to the power and presence of God's reign. (*Missional Church,* p. 159)

Taking Risks as a Contrast Community

LOIS Y. BARRETT

"And even if our gospel is veiled, it is veiled to those who are headed toward destruction. In their case the god of this age has blinded the minds of the unbelievers, to keep them from seeing the light of the gospel of the glory of Christ, who is the image of God. . . . We are afflicted in every way, but not crushed; perplexed, but not driven to despair; persecuted, but not forsaken; struck down, but not destroyed."

(2 Cor. 4:3-4, 8-9)

Pattern: The missional church is learning to take risks for the sake of the gospel. It understands itself as different from the world because of its participation in the life, death, and resurrection of its Lord. It is raising questions, often threatening, about the church's cultural captivity and grappling with the ethical and structural implications of its missional vocation.

When our team first drew up the "indicators of a missional church," risk taking was not on our list. But as we visited the congregations in our sample, it became apparent that many of them were taking risks for the sake of the gospel. The staff of Transfigura-

74

tion Parish took immigrants whom they had never seen before into their homes to live. They continue to do so, even though one man tried to set fire to his room in the rectory. The custodian at Spring Garden decided to let a homeless man live in the garage on the church property. He thought that nobody else in the congregation knew, but they did know about it and were willing to let it happen. The Eastbrook congregation moved their worship site into a neighborhood plagued by drug use and burglaries. They take for granted that the building will be broken into, and equipment will have to be replaced. The Boulder Church contracted to bring the Peace Factory traveling exhibit to the city without knowing where they would get the money for expenses or the volunteers to staff it. The money and the people appeared when they were needed. Franklin Reformed Church of Nutley, New Jersey, in the IMPACT group decided to enter the change process without knowing where the money for the process would come from; another congregation in the group then gave the money for them. Holy Ghost Church says they make decisions on the basis of mission and vision, not whether it is in the budget.

These congregations seem to be living by a set of rules different from that of the dominant culture. Their priorities are different. They act against the "common sense." They are trying to conform to Jesus Christ rather than to the surrounding society.

Second Corinthians 4:3-4 says: "And even if our gospel is veiled, it is veiled to those who are headed toward destruction. In their case, the god of this age has blinded the minds of the unbelievers, to keep them from seeing the light of the gospel of the glory of Christ, who is the image of God" (my translation). In the twenty-first century, the god of this age continues to blind people's minds to the light of Christ. The norms of the dominant culture favor the bottom line, the safer option or managed risk ("what's in it for me?"), the use of violence as a means for problem solving.

In contrast, the congregations in this study have let God shine in their hearts "to give the light of the knowledge of the glory of God in the face of Jesus Christ" (v. 6). They understand themselves as different from the world because they are modeling themselves on Jesus Christ, rather than on the world's heroes.

Second Corinthians 3:18 says it this way: "And all of us, with unveiled faces, seeing the glory of the Lord as though reflected in a mirror, are being transformed into the same image from one degree of glory to another; for this comes from the Lord, the Spirit." Missional churches are letting themselves be transformed into the image of Christ, who in turn is the image of God. They are participating in the life, death, and resurrection of Jesus. In the light of Jesus, they are able to look in a discriminating way at the culture in which they find themselves. At critical points they choose to conform to Jesus Christ rather than to the dominant culture. They become contrast communities that take risks based on gospel priorities, rather than society's priorities.

When a congregation is a contrast community in comparison to the dominant culture, the dominant culture often resists. The afflictions, the perplexities, the persecution, even the suffering of violence mentioned in 2 Corinthians 4:8-9 are sometimes part of the risk of living into the image of Christ. Jesus told his disciples, "Servants are not greater than their master. If they persecuted me, they will persecute you" (John 15:20). The god of this world often blinds people to the light of the gospel. So, when congregations, by their life and ministry, give collective witness to Jesus Christ, they are taking risks — physical, financial, social. When their distinctive conduct goes against the grain of society's norms, they may be looked down on or treated unjustly. When they challenge the powers of the world, the powers may fight back.

In other words, risk taking comes with being a contrast community. When one is living across cultures — for example, the dominant culture and the culture of the church as contrast community — there is always a sense of being uncomfortable, a feeling of continuing tension. The Beatitudes (Matt. 5:1-12) illustrate this. When a community is poor in spirit, in mourning, gentle, hungering and thirsting for righteousness, merciful, pure in heart, and making peace, it will be reviled and persecuted and all kinds of evil will be said against it.

Materialism versus Being Present with the Poor

The people of Transfiguration Roman Catholic Parish in Brooklyn know that their calling is to be present with Christ in the Eucharist and present with the poorest of the poor. This presence with the poor also demands a different lifestyle for those in the congregation who can afford a more affluent lifestyle. That is a struggle for many people in the parish. Even the poorest of new immigrants are lured by the possibility of wealth in *El Norte*. At a meeting of the one English-speaking fraternity during our visit, members shared their struggles with living this vision. Materialism and the lure of wealth catch them at unexpected times. They lean on others in the fraternity in order to be able to honor the poor. The dominant culture honors the wealthy. The people of Transfiguration believe that the poor are much more a blessing than the rich.

Father Bryan Karvelis says, "When you concentrate on being contemplative and with the poor, you really do change — your interests — your lifestyle is radically different. . . . I never worry about money. It's just uncanny the way money comes when you need it. As in the Gospels, it's not worrying about having a purse or extra clothing."

For one whole year, the theme for the retreats of the fraternities' responsibles (the leaders) centered on resisting materialism. The weekend we were there, the Saturday morning discussion around gospel and culture, as well as the Sunday morning homily, dealt with finding people who would commit volunteer time to the church, rather than just seeking to meet their own needs or make more money. The fact that such a discussion happened was an indicator both of the norms of the parish and of the difficulties in always living so that one witnesses against materialism.

Others of the congregations in our study also talked about their witness to an affluent society. Members of the Boulder Mennonite Church struggle with their very secular and very wealthy context. One man commented, "It's hard to be in the midst of an extremely affluent community. This county is in the top 10 in the country in affluence. It is difficult to live here and maintain an ethic of simplicity." A woman in the church added, "I don't know how many other churches in Boulder talk about the economic implications of their lives." Another said, "What's our mission field? Affluent, consumer culture."

First Presbyterian Church of Bellevue also struggles with its context of affluence. One member said, "Right here, two or three blocks from here, there are a lot of problems — high school students without meals" in the midst of a relatively wealthy community. The congregation tries to reach out to both ends of the economic spectrum, but with difficulty. "It's hard to evangelize the wealthy. As long as people have enough money, they think they don't have any needs."

Creative Generosity

The Spring Garden Church in Toronto thrives on risk. They use money as creatively as entrepreneurs do — with creative risk taking and quick responsiveness. They have a budget, but when needs come up, they spontaneously allot money to address them.

When an earthquake hit Colombia, two people from the congregation took off for Colombia, on the basis of an earlier connection with churches there. Without checking with anybody else, the church treasurer wrote them a substantial check for expenses and disaster relief. When they got back, they told everybody what they had done and were hugged.

They take risks with young people and give them major responsibility. Matthew, a member of the church and a senior in high school, wanted to organize a citywide youth rally because he began to see his own high school as a mission field. The church backed the event with $20,000, expecting to get it back from the proceeds of the event. Instead, they lost $11,000. Nevertheless the church plans to finance the next citywide youth rally planned by Matthew. "He learned something the first time," they say.

A company owned by a member of the congregation hires homeless people and street kids to manufacture artificial rock. The company loses money, but the owner sees it as a business motivated by compassion. It is the kind of business that unemployed people could start for themselves, they say. He has had endless problems with the business, but he believes in what he does. The monetary losses are secondary to the opportunity to mentor his employees.

Spring Garden Church has been deliberate about being a contrast to the values of dominant culture — success, individualism. They say they want to look at the values and themes of the culture and then emphasize a gospel-informed life. This is not so much anti-culture — the entrepreneurial spirit is a part of the dominant culture. The contrast is their generosity. They take financial risks not for the sake of their own profit, but for the sake of compassion.

Individualism versus Commitment to Community

The clearest way that Rockridge United Methodist Church is a contrast community is in its witness against individualism. The radical commitment to one another in the church community is in contrast to the dominant culture — and particularly to Oakland, California, where they are located. The mission covenant groups require each member to commit to weekly corporate worship and study, spiritual disciplines, Sabbath keeping, exercise of one's spiritual gifts in the church, and generosity, beginning with a tithe.

Mission Covenant Group members report making decisions concerning issues ranging from parenting styles to vocation based on allegiance to the church and its teachings. Some report that their families of origin do not understand their lifestyle. One family often provides a car to another who needs transportation. Child care is considered a community responsibility. Subsidizing the income of a person involved in local mission is expected. People give up lucrative jobs that would require relocation in favor of jobs that offer less income but more opportunity to live in the community where mission activities take place.

Individualism can exist among congregations as well as among people. Individualism suggests to congregations that they can be free and autonomous entities, creating their own life, ministries, and future. Individualism chews away both at a congregation's dependency on the Holy Spirit and its interdependence with other congregations. The recognition of how individualism had eroded the relationships among congregations and the pastors and leaders of those congregations is, in part what led to the formation of a covenant among seven Reformed Church in America congregations in the Synod of the Mid-Atlantics. The covenant affirmed the importance for all participants to think and behave in new ways in relation to one another. It helped them address issues in relationship, not in isolation from, one another. Through the covenant, they could encourage and support one another's full participation in the Mission Church learning process. The IMPACT design and management team reported to the synod: "Honest, direct communication and intentional surfacing and resolution of conflict have moved us toward more genuine community. Reaching beyond our individualism, we have discovered that, as a 'body,' we are stronger and healthier than the 'collective of individuals' ever was."

Ministry to Those on the Edges of Society

Most of the congregations we visited took risks by ministering to those society has rejected. Bellevue houses a school for high-school dropouts in the church building. Diane, a woman at Spring Garden, has a ministry with women who have been sexually abused or have sexual identity issues as well as with women who are ex-offenders. She herself has served time in prison. She has experienced a lot of support in the congregation for her ministry, even though the women with whom she works are generally uncomfortable in the church because of their marginalization. Diane organizes Spring Garden members to serve as volunteers for "circles" of women that can surround those women being ministered to. She envisions a greater involvement by Spring Garden with AIDS patients and providing a place where evangelicals and gay activists, for example, can meet on common ground.

Transfiguration Parish is located in a neighborhood that is predominantly Hispanic Catholic and Hasidic Jewish. One day Sister Marcy, principal of Transfiguration School, looked out her door to see several Jewish men chasing and then attacking an African-American man who had allegedly stolen something from a Jewish fruit market. She came running out as the police arrived, about to arrest the thief. She told the police, "If you arrest this man, you also have to arrest the ones who are beating him up."

Nonconformity as Witness

When these congregations are contrast communities for the sake of the gospel, they are a public witness to the gospel. They are reflections of God's light, even if those who are blinded by the god of this age, have trouble seeing the light. The church, as different for Christ's sake, is meant to see by the "light of the gospel of the glory of Christ" and to be seen by the world.

People at Transfiguration Parish say, "Social justice is not our main focus." They just concentrate on helping the "poorest of the poor" who come to their door. But people all over New York City know of the work of Transfiguration Parish — the help for immigrants seeking asylum, the hospice for AIDS patients, the Southside Community Mission. Being different for Christ's sake is a public witness.

For some, simply making a public witness is a faithful response to the gospel, even if it does not appear to be immediately effective. One member at Boulder Mennonite Church reflected on the experience of organizing Peace Factory, "At key points a lot of people from the congregation joined in to help it happen. Every regular attender helped somehow. It was encouraging that people would do it. The funny thing is, I don't necessarily think that the time I spent on it was most efficient, because the response in Boulder was not overwhelming. But that's what the gospel's all about. It's not necessarily overwhelming to everybody all the time."

Sharing in the Sufferings of Christ

This nonconformity to the world (and conformity to Christ) sometimes results in suffering, violence against these congregations, or simply strained relationships. Several of these congregations have experienced difficulties with others in their denomination because of the way they do things different. The IMPACT churches took a course of action the rest of their synod had rejected. They have endured the scorn of some of their colleagues, who said, "What are you doing that for?" They have been accused of being a cult. But they are still in the Reformed Church in America. At times relationships between the Spring Garden Church and other Canadian Baptists have not been good. The leaders of the congregation say they are never sure they can get enough Baptist pastors to show up for an ordination council. Other National Baptist churches in Detroit used to see Holy Ghost Full Gospel Baptist Church as a cult because of its expectation that members would actually practice discipleship and holy living.

Boulder Mennonite Church has made its risky public witness in the areas of peace and service. Reconciliation is central to their understanding of the gospel. "If we are faithful Christians, we will be out of step with the culture," says Steve Goering, co-pastor. "The peace position, if it's carried through in a radical way, represents that. It is a discipline and a training for speaking out in other areas. In the Gulf War we were a sanctuary church for a fellow in the Navy who wished to be a conscientious objector. They wouldn't let him out of the military." Because of the church's advocacy for this young man, an anonymous person threw red paint on the church door, and the pastors received nasty phone calls.

Since then, the Boulder Church has also taken risks in local peacemaking. "We have a Christian Peacemaker reserve team," says former pastor Marilyn Miller. "When the riots on the 'hill' [near the University of Colorado] happened, four or five of us called each other. We could not get to the church building [near the university] because the road was blockaded. There were police in riot helmets with guns. We walked the streets, talked to students, shopkeepers, and the police. We did try to help, and we're still going to meetings to keep working at that so it doesn't happen again." The Christian Peacemaker Team members tried to build connections with both students and merchants.

Fellow peacemaker Brenda Ottoman reflected, "It was strange to have this practically martial law on the hill in Boulder. We were walking back from the hill one evening, and I thought we were done. Then there were the cops." Some on the team wondered, Were the police open to talking to them? Were they open to problem solving by nonviolent means? "Marilyn went up to talk to the police about how they saw the situation. I was amazed. The police knew that we were from this church, and it was a great dialogue."

Such congregations might take comfort from 2 Corinthians 4:8-9: *We are afflicted in every way, but not crushed; perplexed, but not given to despair; persecuted, but not forsaken; struck down, but not destroyed.*

But the congregations in our study did not think of the risks they took for the sake of the gospel as all sorrow and struggle. They found joy in their risk taking. As in the parable of the Pearl of Great Price (Matt. 13:45-46), many of them willingly take risks in order to be faithful to Jesus Christ and to be a sign of the reign of God. They also knew the risks of not taking risks for the sake of the gospel, the risk of unfaithfulness, of not relying on God to accomplish what God had called and sent them to do.

The nature of the church's witness to the world is this non-conformed engagement with the world. This engagement happens both through specific words and deeds performed in the world and through the witness of being a presence in the world, different from the world, inviting questions, challenging assumptions, and demonstrating a life not of the world. (*Missional Church,* p. 117)

Practices That Demonstrate
God's Intent for the World

DALE A. ZIEMER

*"We have renounced the shameful things that one hides; we re-
fuse to practice cunning or to falsify God's word, but by the
open statement of the truth we commend ourselves to the conscience of everyone in the sight of God."*

(2 Cor. 4:2)

Pattern: The church's life as a community is a demonstration
of what God intends for the life of the whole world. The practices of the church embody mutual care, reconciliation, loving
accountability, and hospitality. A missional church is indicated
by how Christians behave toward one another.

D ietrich Bonhoeffer in his classic book *Life Together* describes in a
practical way the Christian community as the setting in which
the gospel proclamation materializes, that is, where it can be seen, felt,
heard, and tasted. Where the gospel takes on public and demonstrable
form in the life of the Christian community, life is transformed, united
with Christ, made whole.

The church is responsible for bearing forth the gospel proclamation to the world. It is to manifest that proclamation in a material, physical way through its particular life in community. In, with, and through this community, by its intricate web of relationships and patterns of social behavior, the gospel of the reign of God is declared. The "open statement of truth," to which the apostle Paul refers, is heard believably only where there is a gospel-formed community to manifest it visibly. This visible community exists not for itself, but for God's mission — to be the sign and foretaste of God's reign of justice, freedom, and love.

The gospel is a profound gift and its public demonstration is the challenging call of the entire Christian community, not the vocational option of a select minority within the community. One of the obstacles to the gospel's public demonstration today is the embedded cultural understanding that equates the church with the role, function, and person of the professional minister, pastor, or priest. In the thinking and practice of the churches visited in this study, in a variety of ways the "church" is no longer being identified with clergy services or church programs. Rather, as Bonhoeffer puts it, the church and ministry are becoming understood as "redemptive relationships in community." The Christian communities we visited are learning to become proclaimers of God's word for and to one another.

Our visits uncovered certain patterns of redemptive relationships in community. These patterns, or Christian practices, are communal or social in nature. They point to the manner in which people take time to listen to one another, are actively helpful toward one another, bear with one another, and cross boundaries erected by differences between them. These simple yet profound communal practices are being taught, and people participate in them in ever deepening ways. They contribute essentially to the missional character of the congregation, for they are rooted in the gospel and offer a redemptive contrast to the social patterns of the dominant North American culture. These practices are patterns of communal behavior that form the content of a congregation's "open statement." The practices we observed were intentional, not accidental. Their motivation and character were deeply related to the gospel their churches sought to proclaim.

As we visited these congregations, we did not expect to discover a "full meal," but rather a "foretaste," not an unambiguous manifestation of the reign of God, but a glimpse, a witness to God's active rendering of a new creation in the midst of the old. The churches we visited offer the watching world a varied and flavorful foretaste of God's activity. As Father Bryan Karvelis of Transfiguration Parish said, "We don't have all the fancy first-rate programs, just the experience of being loved." In particular, practical, and diverse ways, these congregations are holding themselves accountable for certain practices that form the distinctive witness of the church in the world. In particular, we saw practices of listening, active helpfulness, and bearing in ways that were at once modest yet profound. All of these practices involve crossing boundaries erected by differences between people and welcoming the "other" who is different from "us" with hospitality. These practices, it seems, did not automatically or naturally spring up, but are being introduced, cultivated, and reinforced in intentional ways.

Listening to One Another

The practice of listening is a fundamental characteristic of churches manifesting "redemptive relationships in community." It is God's work, for when we learn to listen to our sisters and brothers we welcome them as God does. Listening to one another also corresponds with the practice of listening to God, for it involves quieting our self-focused interests and plans.

One of the greatest obstacles to truly listening to one another in our contemporary world is the stricture of heavily scheduled lives. A busy schedule has become a status symbol for contemporary Americans. A growing expectation is that taking time for church means budgeting time for church along with other commitments and priorities. One IMPACT pastor pointed out that even though budgeting time for church sounds like a good thing, it raised a new concern: When some members offer time for church-related work other than worship on Sunday morning, it is seen to take up the time they had budgeted for church that week. "I won't see them at Sunday worship if they were here on Thursday night or Saturday morning."

But in the midst of heavily scheduled lives, a new pattern is emerging in and among IMPACT congregations. Significant sharing and listening is occurring as leaders and members have discovered new and more fruitful patterns of interaction. "How much time does it take to be the church?" became a genuine question along their journey of missional faithfulness. Leaders introduced early and reinforced often the expectation that they would spend time together and that they would talk with and listen to one another in a significant manner. Participatory Bible study brought to the fore key lessons about church. People became liberated from static, minimal notions of church that had held them captive. They discovered the importance of "one-anothering" — ministering to and with one another in a way that often is time intensive. It takes time to talk with one another, to listen to one another, to care for one another, to love one another, to bear with one another, to confess to one another, and to forgive one another. As a result, people who had not spent much time together before began to find it difficult to pull away from the table. Meaningful listening and learning about one another as sisters and brothers in Christ were taking place.

A Transfiguration fraternity illustrates well what is meant by the practice of listening in a culture that so highly values the busy schedule. A fundamental concern for listening to God and to one another guides the interaction in each fraternity meeting. And it takes time. How much time? Fraternities meet weekly on Fridays for the entire evening. The general climate of a fraternity is characterized by nonjudgmental, compassionate, and accepting interaction with one another. The discipline of holding one's tongue, of forgoing analysis and advice, is present in each meeting. Fraternities hold themselves answerable to one another because of the Christian bond among them. Members honor one another as a different person each week is given the floor to share the salient point of the Christian life he or she is dealing with at present. Patient and attentive listening takes place. Members of fraternities participate together in God's work by the manner in which they actively share in a common life. As brothers and sisters in Christ, they take time to listen to one another.

"The fraternities are the primary model of pastoral care," said Father Bryan. Fraternity members agree that the life and energy of the church is found there. Close relationships are forged because of a common Savior and the shared discipleship life to which he calls them. People spend time with each other, care for each other, help each other out of troubles. If the shortage of priests in the Roman Catholic

Church were to touch Transfiguration and result in a lack of priestly services, the fraternities would continue to exist, members believe. The fraternities would then serve as "priest," as they do now, to one another. Even the preaching that Father Bryan does they already do for one another, for teaching, reminding, and exhorting also occur in the fraternities. Without listening, such talk could easily become condescending toward the other, mere pious words. But because members take time for and listen to one another, their conversation is sacramental. In a significant way, they are Christ — living food and drink — for one another.

The practice of listening to one another is learned alongside that of listening to God. At Transfiguration Parish, leaders gather early every Saturday morning for prayer and silent meditation before they deliberate about parish concerns. At Holy Ghost Full Gospel, the elders and pastors expect to meet one another each weekday morning to pray on behalf of the church community and its ministry. At Eastbrook all program and activity is suspended for two weeks each year dedicated to prayer. During this time all are invited to gather daily at 6:00 a.m., noon, and/or 6:30 p.m. for prayer. At Rockridge the path toward accountable discipleship in community involves persons entering into a Listening Covenant Group. The purpose of this group is to listen to God in communion with one another to discern God's grace and call as members of the Body of Christ. In the IMPACT project the primary focus has been on seeking and listening to God in a context of more accountable Christian community to discern God's direction and call for the future. There is significant evidence in the churches we visited that the service of listening to one another and to God go hand in hand; one informs and shapes the practice of the other. There is something innately purposeful about the practice of listening within the context of the congregations visited. It could have to do with Bonhoeffer's observation, "We listen with the ears of God so that we may speak the Word of God."

Active Helpfulness

The concrete manifestation of love often comes in acts of helpfulness to one another. Christians are accountable to one another because "we have this treasure" (2 Cor. 4:7). As members of this new community, they are willing to be interrupted and diverted from their plans by the requests and claims of others, in order that "the life of Jesus may also be made visible" (2 Cor. 4:10) in them. This biblical image of the reign of God offers a vision for human life and community that contrasts sharply with the pattern of individualism that is so common in the dominant North American culture. Individualism elevates the freedom of the individual to believe and do whatever she chooses in the way that best enables her to realize her own happiness. It teaches, "I can do it by myself." Such a view presents a daunting obstacle for the formation of Christian community and authentic patterns of "one-anothering."

Through the practice of active helpfulness, churches are learning how to engage and overcome these barriers. Active helpfulness means individuals will come to know enough about one another to become significantly involved in each other's lives. It means becoming open and honest with one another; sometimes it means confronting, sometimes consoling. The discipline of holiness at Holy Ghost Full Gospel Church has this practical face to it. It challenges the culture's assumption of individual rights and private space in order to participate in God's work of bringing wholeness to relationships and healing to communities. But a pattern of helpfulness requires more than what individuals coming to church to meet their spiritual needs expect. It offers more sometimes than they desire. Communal patterns of active helpfulness require frequent and sustained interaction. How can we be helpful if we do not spend time enough to come to know one another? Active helpfulness involves discovering both the large and small joys as well as knots that entangle one another's lives.

Members of some Rockridge Mission Covenant Groups have deliberately moved into the neighborhood of others in their group. They have done so in order for their families to interact with one another on a more frequent basis. One member of a Mission Covenant Group took a job as a teacher in a needy school near the church. Just after the principal hired him and he had quit his previous teaching position, she informed him that she didn't have the money for his position. His Mission Covenant Group banded together to make up his salary, and together with a matching grant, it reached the amount that he originally had been hired to earn. Although this material sharing is not typical of every group at Rockridge, members are prepared to do this if the opportunity arises. Such action is based on the assumption that they will be radically involved in living life together.

Helpfulness requires the sharing of time, energy, and material or financial resources in simple and modest ways that are not necessarily spectacular. It means being present for one another in small ways as well as in the great moments. One immigrant who came knocking on the rectory door at Transfiguration described how Father Karvelis gave him a blanket, pillow, and sheet. He later exclaimed, "No one had ever been that nice to me before." Father Karvelis's helpful act is merely illustrative of a community where the lack of earthly possessions fails to limit the generosity, kindness, and helpfulness toward one another.

At Spring Garden in Toronto young people in the Christian community engage in ministry with the "squeegee kids" on street corners by bringing them soft drinks and sandwiches. If asked where they're from, they answer, "We're from a church nearby. This is for Jesus." This ministry grows out of the thoughtful consideration of parents and adults who are taking the time to become deeply involved with their own young people. "Our point is to build a sense of responsibility, to help our children become exposed to others in the name of Jesus (to learn and not just to give handouts), to help them get connected with others not like them whom God loves. This is definitely a church where we are a family and really care about each other."

Alfred Loisy once said, "Jesus proclaimed the kingdom, and what came was the church." This statement often has been taken to be an indictment of the church. But, in fact, it points to the critical connection between the life of the church and the proclamation of the reign of God. There is an assumption evident in the churches that we visited that there is to be a connection between what the church says and what it does. The patterns of active helpfulness indicate missional faithfulness because the small deeds are seen to be connected to the proclamation. Congruence between the church's talk and its walk are expected. A member of Boulder Mennonite Church shared this story: "I moved three or four times this past year, and these are the people who carried my boxes and packed my china. They go beyond vocalizing to action. It really happens." And another said, "We've had a number of deaths in the congregation. When our son Michael died in southwestern Colorado in an accident, people were there for us. People from the church paid [pastors] Susan and Steve's way to join us there. At Michael's funeral I thought about this. That's what the church is all about. I can't imagine going through that without the church family." God's love and mercy are proclaimed joyfully and convincingly not in the abstract, but in communities characterized by deeds of love and mercy in everyday active helpfulness.

Bearing with One Another

As believers make the time and space to listen to and help one another, they will begin to know each other in a way that moves beyond the superficial nature of most social interactions. They will encounter difficulties. Rather than sidestepping the burdens others may impose upon them, those in community in and through Jesus Christ become involved in bearing with one another.

This is most dramatically seen in the story of Anne Pilsbury, an attorney and director of Transfiguration's immigration office. "We at Transfiguration believe that Christ calls us to be present to God and present to the poorest of the poor. The hardest thing about that is that it means you lose control of your life. You take what comes. You don't know what you'll face. I couldn't do this work without knowing I was in the heart of a Christian community where people — the community — recognized the suffering of the poor." Anne came to work at Transfiguration in the poor district of Williamsburg in Brooklyn from a law office on Manhattan. At first she wanted to keep a foot in both worlds — one among the poor of Brooklyn through her professional work in the parish's immigration office and the other in her familiar and comfortable world. But at Transfiguration, she quickly became intimately involved in people's suffering. She became immersed in continually painful court battles. "We are a part of so many tragedies here," she said. The work of Transfiguration's immigration office is characterized by the service of bearing and involves personal sacrifice. The Christian community that demonstrates the "open statement of the truth" — that Jesus Christ has "borne our griefs" — is characterized by the actual service of bearing with one another. To experience life in Christ is to experience nothing less than the burden of the other.

At Boulder Mennonite Church a child who was born with complicating birth defects was dying. Half the congregation showed up to make a music tape for him and his family. The ministry of bearing is love in action, sharing and dealing with the issues that touch and shape people's lives most deeply. Because of Christ, the pattern of the Christian life is indicated by "humility and gentleness, with patience, bearing with one another in love" (Eph. 4:2).

At Spring Garden Church, members invest in faith ventures that are stimulated through the life of the community. In one instance, a youth group member sought the congregation's support for launching a Toronto citywide youth gathering. Members invested financially to support this promising ministry. But the venture failed to break even — in fact, it failed to do so by many thousands of dollars. Yet by no means was it perceived to be a failure; rather it was seen as a learning experience for the young man who organized it. It is a pattern that members of Spring Garden joyfully bear one another's burdens — even their economic losses — in very material ways.

Crossing Boundaries, Welcoming the "Other"

The concept of "redemptive relationships in community" has validity and relevance only when it does not gloss over the real challenges of living in community. Actual practices of listening, helpfulness, and bearing all involve crossing real boundaries and overcoming real barriers that separate people from each other. This is hospitality: where listening, helpfulness, and bearing do not turn away from but instead confront difference and engage the other-ness of those who are other than ourselves. These practices offer a challenge to our familiar worlds, while they also transform us. Where patterns of boundary-crossing behavior exist, the missional faithfulness of congregations is being formed. The Christian community is taking on the character of the coming reign of God.

Transfiguration Parish, for example, is typified by great diversity-in income levels, in the length of time spent in the United States, in nationalities, and in languages. In one fraternity alone there are Mexican, Puerto Rican, Anglo, Dominican, and Nicaraguan persons. When fraternities join with other fraternities in annual retreat a common question is, What country are you from? People are constantly crossing paths with people who are not like them, and in this the world has a foretaste of God's promised future.

Crossing boundaries at Boulder Mennonite Church has the fundamental purpose of reconciling differences. Reconciliation is central to their understanding and demonstration of the gospel. In this congregation, five or six persons are members of a Christian Peacemaker reserve team. During the riots in Boulder in 1997, this team brought a third presence — a reconciling one — to the situation.

In sites we visited, the habit of welcoming the stranger or visitor into the community was frequently observed. At Boulder Mennonite Church the motivation for welcoming visitors into the worshiping community is not based on their new-member potential. Visitors report that they feel welcomed but not recruited. "There was genuine interest in who I was and what I had to offer, not so much getting me as a body into the church," said one who has recently become part of the community.

Welcoming the visitor at Eastbrook is based on the assumption that the person new to Christ and the Christian community deserves the very best of the congregation's attentiveness. Even problematic persons are welcomed. One Sunday morning a member of the congregation, a professional actor, entered the worship service playing the part of a homeless man, coming only to look for his friend Ernie (an actual member of the congregation). In character, he was hoping that someone might tell him where he could find Ernie, because Ernie had befriended him. "Ernie befriended me because of Jesus," the homeless man said. He wanted to meet this Jesus, too, and wondered if anyone could help him do that. But, before this drama even began to unfold, as the actor was "getting into his character" and before his real identity was revealed to anyone, he received several invitations to dinner by members of the congregation!

The outcast and the marginalized are drawn into the circle of the community of Transfiguration Parish. It happens regularly yet spontaneously. Father Bryan or Sister Marcy (who is principal of Transfiguration Elementary School) and Sister Peggy (who works with immigrants) take in strangers, often new immigrants, to live at the rectory or the convent. "Sometimes we get people who are mentally sick. We have had some hair-raising experiences. You have to be willing to stick your neck out." Listening involves not only offering one's ear but one's living space, a bed, meals, and an address. Transfiguration has a history of taking risks to welcome the "other" and offer the space for fostering redemptive relationships in community. Only once was someone turned away. Father Bryan reported, "One guy finally broke every rule in the house. Something told me, 'Go to his room.' He had set fire to it. So we told him he had to leave."

In one instance, members of several Mission Covenant Groups at Rockridge decided to build a multi-unit dwelling in the city where they would live next to each other and could interact closely. But the interaction they desired was not limited to those whom they knew. It spilled out in a desire to bear the gospel into their wider locale. The group invited an architect to design the structure in such a way that, in contrast to the conventional locked and gated communities, it would be inviting to strangers wandering through.

Frequently, congregational ministry separates groups of people from one another, gathering them into homogeneous groups. The youth group, singles group, young married couples, and seniors groups are sometimes examples of this. At Boulder Mennonite Church, however, there is a different pattern. "We don't have a large youth group. Kids are not segregated off somewhere. But there is quality interaction between adults and kids."

Lowering the barriers of difference and showing hospitality is perhaps most difficult when someone in the community is wronged by another. Wherever people know a great deal about each other, they also become more aware of their differences. In these situations the probability of conflict exists. Here, crossing boundaries and welcoming the other is a nice concept, but is difficult to practice. At Rockridge, for example, Mission Covenant groups recognize the likelihood of conflict. They indicate they are neither surprised nor completely at a loss when it occurs. When a wrong is done to another, reconciliation is expected that includes confessing to and forgiving each other.

At Holy Ghost Full Gospel Baptist Church, real conflicts between people are a matter of concern, prayer, and action of the faith community. This pattern contrasts with the cultural norm that suggests interpersonal conflicts are a private matter and really no one else's business. But this cultural pattern limits the possibility of reconciliation. When the church accommodates this cultural norm, the opportunity to manifest the reconciliation of God's coming reign is lost. Redemptive relationships are no longer a possibility. Holy Ghost Church is undaunted by the privatism that invades and holds many congregations captive. This community, for example, recognizes that holiness is not a matter of private piety but is essentially social in nature. Love has to do with all social relationships. In one instance, a couple with a failing marriage in the congregation summoned the prayers, support, and counsel of fellow members. Some became deeply involved with the couple and helped them to bridge their differences and reconcile with one another. Assisting one another to cross the barriers of difference, especially when manifested in conflict situations, demonstrates God's intent for the life of the world. Here is an "open statement of the truth," a visible declaration that all creation was meant to live in reconciled relationships.

Before the Watching World

"Jesus came into Galilee, proclaiming the good news of God and saying, 'The time is fulfilled, and the kingdom of God has come near'" (Mark 1:14-15). Here Mark introduces the beginning of the public ministry of Jesus. The reign of God was becoming manifest through the life, instruction, and preaching of Jesus and the common life of the disciple community he formed around himself. There is evidence in the New Testament communities that followed that life together "in Christ" was purposeful, intended to manifest before the watching world the promise and possibilities of the coming age. Thus for the apostle Paul, how life together is conducted in this new community is as important as the content of its proclamation. "We refuse to practice cunning or to falsify God's word, but by the open statement of the truth we commend ourselves to the conscience of everyone in the sight of God" (2 Cor. 4:2).

Through our visits we have seen glimpses of the social reality that Jesus proclaimed, taught, and lived among his disciples. Not unambiguous evidences, but glimmers nevertheless. God's reign of justice, truth, and love both assumes and forms a particular community. One IMPACT pastor indicated, "We are beginning to understand that it is not our programs or projects, but that our life together is representative of something."

We have seen this in practices that are characterized by accountable listening, helpfulness, and bearing with one another, so that the faith community represents Christ, offers Christ, and is Christ for the redemption of life in today's world. In the faith communities we visited, people are getting to know one another as brothers and sisters in Jesus Christ, a new identity that crosses the boundaries that differences erect. They are learning how to engage one another in this new relatedness, proclaiming and embodying the Word as their daily lives interact closely. In their midst, an atmosphere of commitment, trust, and solidarity is forming. Rather than a gathering of strangers, they are devoted to each other's growth and well-being as they pray, worship, study, and serve together. The manner in which they are doing all of this offers to the watching world an impression of the reign of God.

The simple but profound practices described are related at heart to the community's public proclamation of God's Word of salvation. As Dietrich Bonhoeffer asks, "If not accompanied by worthy listening, how can it really be the right word for the other person? If contradicted by one's own lack of active helpfulness, how can it be a convincing and sincere word? If it issues, not from a spirit of bearing and forbearing, but from impatience and desire to force acceptance, how can it be the liberating and healing word?" (*Life Together* [New York: Harper & Row, 1954], p. 25). The importance that such practices have to the gospel proclamation is evidenced most of all by how believers hold themselves accountable to one another for their performance.

The Mission Covenant Groups of Rockridge, a prime example, are patterned after the Wesley class meeting. The purpose of the class meeting was to provide the context of Christian fellowship in which the members would be accountable to one another for their discipleship. The class meeting is an important aspect of United Methodist heritage, one that led to religious renewal in England in the eighteenth century. In the class meeting, men and women came together to pray, to receive exhortation, and to watch over one another in love. John Wesley, who developed the practice, said,

> It can scarce be conceived what advantages have been reaped from this little prudential regulation. Many now happily experienced that Christian fellowship of which they had not so much as an idea before. They began to "bear one another's burdens," and naturally to "care for one another." As they had daily a more

intimate acquaintance with, so they had a more endeared affection for, each other. And "speaking the truth in love, they grew up into him in all things, who is the Head, even Christ." ("A Plain Account of the People Called Methodists," 1748)

Mission Covenant Groups at Rockridge invite people to share in the realities of the pilgrimage of faith. Participants in such groups are constantly attuned to what fellow group members are facing. They are in the habit of making themselves available to one another and watching over one another in love. For these practices they hold themselves accountable. They share a radical commitment to one another that is unheard of amidst the individualism of the wider society.

But what of this radical commitment to "one-anothering" does the world see? Are these sightings visible only to those who are looking for them? Are they visible to general onlookers? The visitation method our team devised was to have also included the observations of those who were acquainted with but not participating in the church's life. But interviews that would have captured this witness of the "watching world" did not take shape as we would have liked. However, there are indications of the public witness that are worth mentioning. It is likely, for example, that Transfiguration Parish is not exercising great influence on the growing and dominant Hasidic Jewish community intermingled among the poor in the Williamsburg part of Brooklyn. But it is not unnoticed. Transfiguration members are sometimes called upon during the Sabbath to come inside a Hasidic house to turn off a light switch or to perform another small act of work. Intent on entering into no one's debt, the Hasidic insist on offering something in return. But, refusing to take any payment, the Christians from Transfiguration point out that their kindness is freely offered. Another example at Transfiguration is Anne, the director of immigration services, who came to that position with no intention of participating further in the life of the parish. She reported that early in her work she was struck by a church whose actions matched its beliefs: she was drawn to attend Mass, and in time became part of a fraternity.

Is the world watching? In North America the dominant culture is less aware and cares even less about the church today than in times past. The "watching world" is less attentive than we may like to think. But in very particular ways the world is watching. The Boulder congregation, for example, would often employ a tow truck service to remove cars, often belonging to university students, illegally parked in the church's small parking lot. Gene was the tow truck operator frequently called. He became impressed by the manner of the congregation in dealing with the shenanigans connected with those illegally parked (for example, a beer bash in a sport-utility vehicle with a portable hot tub). One day Gene stepped inside the church building and said, "I think we need God a little more in our lives. We're wondering if it's okay to visit your church." His wife joined the church after that. Gene hasn't, but he stays connected. The congregation continues its witness. When he developed cancer, the congregation helped to complete construction on his horse barn.

In the neighborhood of Holy Ghost Full Gospel Church, Luther was watching. Luther unhesitatingly described himself as a "big time drunk." He was the ringleader for street residents who found solace in alcohol. He represented one of the most difficult segments of the neighborhood — the men — to reach with the good news of Christ. But something happened when Luther saw people taking over the use of what was to become the church building. He noticed they came in the evening, and when they did he would help direct traffic outside. Then he helped women get to their cars safely in the evening. Eventually he came into the lobby. Then he went as far as the door of the sanctuary. Soon his pattern of drinking changed. Then he was baptized. All the programs and techniques created to reach people like Luther came up short. "Our efforts didn't work, the Holy Spirit did it," people said. Luther was watching. The Holy Spirit brought him to a community that was intentionally formed to be welcoming at every stage and at every door, no strings attached.

One of the important contributions of this study of missional faithfulness has been to identify evidences of new patterns in the midst of the old. The patterns we have seen and cited are becoming the characteristic way of life in the congregations, even as the congregations struggle with other unproductive and less faithful patterns and traditions. These new practices are seen as essential to the gospel proclamation as the "principalities and powers" still wage their warfare. They are taught, and reciprocally, they teach those who participate in them what it means to be the church. These social patterns are cultivated intentionally by the attention given to them by leaders, by the structures that ensure their continued growth and development.

About such practices Bonhoeffer said,

> When God was merciful, when He revealed Jesus Christ to us as our Brother, when He won our hearts by His love, this was the beginning of our instruction in divine love. When God was merciful to us, we learned to be merciful with one another. When we received forgiveness instead of judgment, we too, were made ready to forgive each other. What God did to us, we then owed to others. Thus God taught us to meet one another as God has met us in Christ. (*Life Together*, p. 25)

These words point to God's initiating action toward the world as the motivation and model for redemptive relationships in community. "The community of God reflects the character of God," repeats the pastor at Eastbrook. God's action toward the world is intended to be the recipe for life and ministry of the church. To an observable degree, it is becoming reflected in the tone and quality of the congregations we visited.

> However they take shape, these practices not only form and guide the internal life of the community but also define the church's action within the world. Witnessing to God's creative intent for all humanity, they model and thus proclaim a different way of life to a watching world. (*Missional Church*, p. 182)

Pattern 5

The Public Witness of Worship

LINFORD L. STUTZMAN AND GEORGE R. HUNSBERGER

> *"For we do not proclaim ourselves; we proclaim Jesus Christ as Lord. . . . For it is the God who said, 'Let light shine out of darkness,' who has shone in our hearts to give the light of the knowledge of the glory of God in the face of Jesus Christ."*
>
> (2 Cor. 4:5-6)

Pattern: Worship is the central act by which the community celebrates with joy and thanksgiving both God's presence and God's promised future. Flowing out of its worship, the community has a vital public witness.

M issional worship is neither inwardly directed, meant to satisfy the participants, nor outwardly directed, intended to attract and evangelize the unchurched. Missional worship is God-directed. Marva Dawn writes:

> I am convinced that we should be using new music and new worship forms; however, we should use them not to attract people, but because they are faithful in praising God and forming us to be his people. . . . Good worship will be evangelistic, but that is

not its primary purpose, for it is directed toward God, not toward the neighbor. (*Christian Century,* April 21-28, 1999, p. 455)

Often, traditional congregations with a developing missional vision struggle to create fresh and attractive worship forms in order to draw in new members, while at the same time keep traditionalists happy — a difficult agenda. The early journey of the Rockaway Church, one of the New Jersey IMPACT churches, illustrates that. The initial impetus toward developing a missional direction took the form of innovations in worship. They worked hard to hold both traditionalists and innovators together within the congregation, while also trying to bridge differences of ethnicity, socioeconomic status, generation, and personal taste. Originally Rockaway took the route of having two different kinds of services in order to give members the opportunity to divide along lines of worship style preference. It was an attempt to provide those in each self-selecting group something to which they were attracted, or something with which they would be comfortable. They were seeking both to affirm tradition and to reach out to unchurched persons in the community.

But what became clear was that implementing such style changes in worship to attract some while satisfying others would not necessarily produce a missional congregation. While this model may have seemed at the time to be the only possibility for introducing change while retaining those who opposed it, it created difficulties that continued to absorb a great deal of energy at Rockaway. And in the end, the attempt had limited evangelistic effect. The people with the original vision for evangelistic worship at Rockaway recognize today that so-called contemporary worship — indeed any particular worship style — does not necessarily get at the root issues.

In fact, style of worship or style of music or even quality of music did not seem to be important at all in terms of the missional character of the congregations we visited. Of the churches we observed, some had lively contemporary music; some had high-quality classical music; some had tepid music led by an uncertain choir. One congregation had no hymnals because they couldn't afford them; the parishioners learned the songs by rote just before the service began. People were clearly there for some reason other than the music.

It is flawed thinking to evaluate worship primarily for its ability to attract or satisfy. What is evident among the churches we visited is that they are driven by a deeper conception of worship and its relationship to mission. Among them, we saw a great variety of styles and elements in worship: traditional liturgy, rock music, meditation, drama, dancing. All are ways these congregations remember the death and resurrection of Jesus, celebrate the presence of the Spirit, and anticipate God's reign. Context certainly affects their choices, but their instincts move them away from using worship to attract or recruit people, or using it to satisfy the tastes and preferences of people. Such worship would be just that — worship that is being *used!* Used for some ulterior purpose, worship becomes devalued, a tool to perform some function, an instrument for something other than what it *is*.

Worship is by its very nature God-directed. And understood that way, its relation to the missional character becomes more apparent. Thomas Schattauer, a Lutheran professor of worship, has shown this in a forceful way. He suggests that there are three possible approaches to the relationship between worship (liturgy) and mission. The first he calls "inside and out." This "conventional" approach understands worship as the primary activity that takes place *inside* the church community, and mission as the activity that takes place on the *outside*. In this understanding, "worship nurtures the individual and sustains the community in its life before God and in its life together, and from there Christians go out to serve the church's mission as proclaimers and doers of the gospel" ("Liturgical Assembly as Locus of Mission," in *Inside Out: Worship in an Age of Mission*, ed. by Thomas H. Schattauer [Minneapolis: Fortress Press, 1999], p. 4). So worship empowers those inside the church to take up the mission outside. The difficulty with this approach, Schattauer warns, is that worship is implied to be an instrument to serve mission, even if indirectly so. And in the end, worship and mission remain distinct activities. This view has a long heritage.

A second approach, "outside in," is what Schattauer says is a contemporary response to the conventional model. The "outside" activities of mission are brought into the context of worship.

> The sacred precinct of the liturgy becomes one of two things — either a stage from which to present the gospel and reach out to the unchurched or irreligious, or a platform from which to issue the call to serve the neighbor and rally commitment for social and political action. (p. 4)

Strategies of church growth and social activism alike may reflect this approach. In either case, the instrumental way of seeing worship is even stronger, and more direct, than in the conventional view.

A third approach, the one Schattauer commends, would be to see the relationship as "inside out." This approach locates worship within the larger scope of God's reconciling mission toward the whole world, a mission into which the church is immersed by baptism. So then, "the visible act of assembly (in Christ by the power of the Spirit) and the forms of this assembly — what we call liturgy — enact and signify this mission. From this perspective, there is no separation between liturgy and mission." Schattauer concludes that "the assembly for worship *is* mission" (p. 5).

So to keep the focus of worship on God and to resist the temptation to do otherwise is precisely the missional calling of the church. The churches we visited illustrate this "inside out" approach. Transfiguration Parish shows it when they are concerned to have in their sanctuary a simple symbol of Christ's cross instead of a clutter of ornate and elaborate symbols that bear little correspondence to their calling to be present with the poorest of the poor. Eastbrook Church shows it when they begin worship with a cordial welcome to all who may be visiting, but with a direct and polite invitation for any who are members of other local churches to take Eastbrook's greeting back to their church and pastor. They are convinced that if their worship is toward God, and if that God has come in Jesus Christ for the reconciliation of the world, and if that God has called "one holy catholic and apostolic church" to be joined to that mission, then worship is not for recruiting, and competition between churches is a violation.

The Worship of God as Public Witness

From earliest recorded history, worship was a public act, often connected with politics, the social order, war, economics, prosperity, and power. Worship was public performance of the deepest assumptions about reality held by a particular social group. There was nothing private about fertility rites done in "high places," slaughtering bleating animals then burning them on outdoor altars, dragging a tabernacle through the wilderness. Historically, worship is the glue that holds families, tribes, nations, and empires together. Worship differentiates groups of people from one another. Worship publicly reveals the hidden foundations of cultures and subcultures.

The biblical record of the Hebrew people in Egypt demonstrates the central role and the power of worship to transform a slave community into a nation by enabling this community publicly to reject both the religion and the oppression of their Egyptian masters. Passover, with its blood on the doorposts for all to see, with its open feasting in the middle of the night, anticipates, then later celebrates and reenacts the historical event of liberation. This event originated in worship and culminated in a collective escape from slavery and a journey in the direction of the vision, the promise, the hope, and the Land.

This act of liberating worship was not only a one-time event that religiously, emotionally, culturally, politically and geographically separated the Israelite slaves from their oppressors. For the Israelites in the wilderness and ever since, the Passover ritual was a public acknowledgment of God as the source of the liberation, the present life, and the future hope in this historical event. Passover was, and still remains, the publicly performed story of God's mighty deeds, a story that motivates the celebrants, living between memory and hope, to keep moving ahead in faith toward the promise. The Passover worship event, in its original and early meaning, constituted a statement of reality that clearly had historical, political, and cultural consequences: "Yahweh alone is God," it attested. "We are God's people. God will save us, sustain us, and bring us into the Land of Promise."

Christian worship forms itself around Jesus and the "exodus" that he accomplished in his crucifixion and resurrection. Central to it has been the Lord's Supper, or Eucharist, instituted at Passover and in many ways like it. The Lord's Supper is worship, a ritual participation in the story of the Lord's death (the memory of liberation), and his presence now (the reality of the living Lord among his people) until he comes again (the promise and hope of a future completion). As the events on the day of Pentecost underscored, the empowering presence of the Holy Spirit inspired a public proclamation of the significance of Jesus' death and resurrection, his sacrifice and lordship, his presence and coming again. The Pentecost event had revolutionary effects similar to those of the Exodus and the subsequent Passover remembrances of it. The fledgling Christian community became a worshiping community, recalling the recent memory of Jesus and waiting in expectation for the realization of the reign of God. We read, by the end of Acts 2, that the Pentecost community

> devoted themselves to the apostles' teaching and fellowship, to the breaking of bread and the prayers. . . . Day by day, as they spent much time together in the temple, they broke bread at home and ate their food with glad and generous hearts, praising God and having the goodwill of all the people. And day by day the Lord added to their number those who were being saved. (Acts 2:42, 46-47)

At its heart, the public worship that developed within the early church following Pentecost was revolutionary, public, and powerful in liberating the worshipers from the shaping power of dominant culture. It attracted and incorporated new believers into the community. It gave the community a new identity.

Perhaps what is most telling about the way the early church saw the *public* nature of its life, witness, and worship is its choice of language to describe these things. As has often been noted, the Greek word chosen by the church for its self-description was *ekklesia,* the word for a "public assembly." Other words for distinctly "religious" groups of one sort or another were readily available. Most groups so designated were private club-like cults or groups that followed some secret path to salvation. It is noteworthy that none of these more private notions were used by the church about itself. Instead, it used a term meaning "the ones called out into public assembly." It was a term that connoted something like a town meeting. As God calls the whole world to its proper worship in public assembly, we can think of the church as the community that has thus far assembled. It lives its life, therefore, in public and for the public.

Another important New Testament word has public character: *kerygma.* It was a word for the public announcement made by a herald who spoke on authority of one who sent the message by royal decree. Jesus' proclamation and the church's are of that sort. The word conveys not only the authority of the proclamation but its intended public audience: Here is news for the world.

The same public character is found in one of the New Testament words for worship, *leitourgia,* from which we derive our English word *liturgy.* The word joins together the Greek words for "people" (*laos,* laity) and "work" *(ergon).* In classical usage, the word indicated "a work done for the people," in other words, something like a "public works project" on behalf of the *polis,* the city. The public nature of the word was especially emphatic. The word was used to translate Old Testament descriptions of cultic "service" rendered by priests and Levites. But its use in the New Testament signals a shift. It denotes the "spiritual worship" of Christians, that worship conceived in noncultic ways (Rom. 12:1-2). Paul is the example: he was a minister of Christ, carrying out his "priestly liturgical action" of proclaiming, so that the Gentiles might become an offering pleasing to God (Rom. 15:16). All believers are now "capable of emulating this 'noncultic' priesthood" and "their *leitourgia,* in imitation of Christ's, is a life poured out in the service of God and humanity" (Mark R. Francis, CSV, "Liturgy," in *Dictionary of Mission,* ed. by Müller, Sundermeier, Bevans, and Bliese [Maryknoll, N.Y.: Orbis Books, 1999], pp. 284-85).

So we have these three:

> *ekklesia:* an assembly gathered for decision making, a town meeting
> *kerygma:* a public proclamation heralded in the name of one who has ultimate authority
> *leitourgia:* a public works project, works on behalf of the people and their public good

The church as a community, the church's message, and the church's worship are all cast in the most public of language. Worship is public witness. And everything it does — when we look closely at its effects and consequences on participants and onlookers alike — has a public horizon. This is what is so inherently missional about worship.

Worship Declares God's Reign

Worship — if we hear what we're saying and watch what we're doing — is a declaration of allegiance over against the present order. In one way or another, a declaration of God's reign is latent in the language and actions of just about all Christian worship. If the Scriptures are read, the story of God's coming to reign is told. If hymns or praise songs are sung, the psalter's acclamations of God as ruler are echoed. If sins are confessed and pardon assured, the good news of God's reign is received. If baptism and the Lord's Supper are celebrated, the reign of God is shown to be at hand. Whatever else may be happening, the words and actions of worship declare that God rules, in Jesus Christ, through the power of the Holy Spirit.

In the churches we visited, we detected that, and something more. Noting the presence of the language of the reign of God in the words and songs and rituals does not in and of itself identify the missional consciousness of these congregations. What we noticed were signs that these churches were *attentive* to the seriousness of such a declaration. They realized how declaring God's reign declares a contrasting way of interpreting the world, a way of interpreting things that contests all other interpretations. They are learning to recognize their worship to be a declaration of allegiance on their part. They yield themselves to this alternative regime and celebrate it as the world's only hope.

In some of the churches we visited, this takes the form of a deliberate, prophetic witness over against some public policy or practice or proposal for public action seen as counter to the claims of God. For example, the Boulder Church engages in direct political action that "grows directly out of its identity and contrast with the world," expressed in worship, that acclaims there is no other god than the God and Father of Jesus Christ. During the student riots on the hill in Boulder, members of the congregation walked among the police and the rioters attempting to talk to people in an effort to diffuse the violence. Another deliberate effort to speak and demonstrate the gospel within a violent culture is the Boulder Church's ongoing involvement with the Christian Peacemaker Teams. The congregation also sponsored the "Peace Factory," an interactive display that prophetically confronts the culture of violence that shapes Americans, including Christians.

Transfiguration's relentless concern for the poorest of the poor and the marginalized is an indirect but potent indictment of the cherished American myths of limitless individual economic opportunity, of economic and social justice, and of the inevitable rewards of hard work. Sunday after Sunday, in the Eucharist — itself a powerful symbol of Christ's own poverty and suffering — congregants are present with God in contemplative prayer and "present with heart and soul and body with the poor." The worshipers are reminded that the world they experience is in need of redemption. It is not the kingdom of God. The inherent injustices and fallenness of the systems within the dominant culture are routinely exposed in their worship.

In other churches we visited, the form is less direct and perhaps more apolitical, focusing on meeting the needs of people victimized or injured by the dominant values, desires, or policies of the general public. First Presbyterian Church of Bellevue invests its time and resources in this direction. They support a program for high school completion for dropouts from the public education system. The scope of their youth ministry enfolds teenagers from a variety of socioeconomic backgrounds and from homes beyond those of the church. They share involvement with other churches in food bank, soup kitchen, and affordable housing ministries, both in the core of the city as well as in surrounding areas. Even though there is a tendency for faith to be understood primarily in individualistic ways, the social implications of that faith are consistently stressed. Bible studies for businesspeople envision not only bringing people to faith in Jesus Christ but enabling them to work out the implications of Christ's lordship in their work worlds.

While Spring Garden Church is becoming surrounded by "monster" or "trophy" houses, it stubbornly refuses to let itself and the neighborhood forget that "the poor are always with us." Albert, the custodian, gives shelter to a homeless man in a garage on the church property. The congregation practices prayer walks and public worship on the streets. These acts of worship are at once prophetic protests of the status quo, and learning opportunities for the participants to see the effects of sin within the flawed social structures of which they are a part.

In at least one church we visited, Eastbrook, there was nervousness about being thought to be "political." But even this congregation's actions make obvious its members' awareness of the disjuncture between the dominant culture and the reign of God. Their worship is deeply saturated with music drawn from a variety of ethnic and national backgrounds. This is by intention and conviction. The church, while having a majority of Anglo members, is also home to numerous people of Hispanic, Asian, and African descent. The church has been especially welcoming to recent immigrant populations in the city. So when on occasion there are multiple national flags displayed in the sanctuary during worship, this is not merely a gesture indicating where Eastbrook has sent missionaries. It represents their own multiple national origins and the nations within which they have sister churches with whom they have cultivated relationships. The American flag is on those occasions displayed alongside the other flags, but it is not prominent or otherwise present in the worship place. This is at once a rejection of nationalism and a declaration of allegiance to Jesus' lordship that transcends all national identities and unifies the diverse human family into one new community of faith.

In worship, there is always something of a contest going on. A worshiping community places itself in the middle of that. Whose story do we take to be the true picture of how things are? Under which regime will we live? In the North American setting, there are many versions of reality being presented, and many claims made upon our loyalty. The missional dimension of a church's life comes to focus when it is recognized in worship how much the gospel is at odds with the going commitments of the culture. Michael Warren illustrates that by looking at how forceful consumerism has become in our society. "When worshipers who have ingested the religion of consumerism bring it unnamed and unrecognized into the place of worship, we have a radical conflict between two claims of ultimacy, the overt one of a formal religion and the covert one of the consumerism faith." But, on the other hand, he says, "When a community enters worship in touch with the message of Jesus and its deep contestation of the consumer ethos, the act of worship celebrates the gospel in a way that itself radically contests that ethos" (*At This Time, In This Place: The Spirit Embodied in the Local Assembly* [Harrisburg, Pa.: Trinity Press International, 1999], p. 18). The counterconsumerist lifestyle choices of the Boulder Church and some of the Rockridge Mission Covenant Groups loom large as acts of worship when this is understood.

Worship Sustains the Identity of the Christian Community

The church is called to have a different political identity from the people around it. The symbol of the church's alternative identity is worship. In its most concrete origins, the Hebrew word for *worship* denotes the physical act of falling down on one's face on the ground in homage before one's ruler. Thus God the Ruler is at the center of the church's worship. The praise and prayer of worship, the reading and preaching of Scripture, the fellowship around the table, and the washing of baptism that initiates new citizens of heaven — all these define an alternative community with an alternative allegiance. (*Missional Church,* p. 119)

One of our friends and colleagues, Craig Van Gelder, has frequently said that in North America the Sunday worship hour has become a *substitute* for the church. That tendency is subverted and set right by the way Transfiguration Parish sees things. For them, worship expresses "the community that is already there; you cannot make community in worship." "Ritual," says Father Bryan Karvelis of Transfiguration Parish, "doesn't have any meaning unless you are living it." Participants experience the weekly meetings of the fraternities as the place where the life of the community is nurtured through close fellowship and by reviewing their lives of discipleship together. The Saturday morning gathering of the responsibles includes contemplation of the Eucharist, in which, Father Bryan says, "we are present to God in quiet, silent, long, contemplative prayer." The Sunday Mass, then, is worship in which that communal life is publicly and collectively celebrated.

That Sunday Mass plays a crucial role in the life and mission of the community. "Ritual reinforces your living. It's not how stimulating or inspiring or energetic the music is that changes us. Rather, worship expresses a profoundly distinct worldview. The worldview expressed in worship and the experience of the people must correspond." The unique worship of Transfiguration did not produce the changes in the life of the church over the last 40 years. Rather, it accompanied and contributed to the life of the church in the world.

There is a wonderful paradox in all of this. The church is called to worship God and to do it in public view. Its worship is not about itself, but about God. The people of God don't approach worship for what they can get out of it. In worship, they are called instead to give something to God: their adoration, their confession, their faith, their loyalty, and their obedience. And yet, by worshiping that way, their identity as the people of God is being formed! They are being formed as Christ's disciples, personally and corporately.

The churches we visited give attention to how they shape the expressions of worship they will give to God. It is also true of them that worship shapes their identity as Christian churches in this postmodern Western culture by nurturing and sustaining those things in their life and witness that distinguish what is good news about the gospel. As in the celebration of Passover by the Hebrews in the wilderness, worship reflects what the congregation already is, and makes the congregation what it is becoming. God's liberated people both shape and are shaped by their worship. As an architect once noted, when you are designing a new house, you are in a sense shaping your world. But once you move into it, from then on it shapes your world.

The very act of worship can function to declare the identity of a Christian community. The gatherings for worship frequently stand in sharp contrast to the normal public routines of life in a particular neighborhood. Even the church facilities to which the faithful flock on Sunday morning for worship, like the tabernacle in the wilderness, or the cathedral in a European city, publicly and continuously announce the presence of the worshiping community throughout the week. In some cases, well-maintained or newly renovated facilities, or facilities with nontraditional symbols, present a marked contrast in the midst of decay and ruin in the surrounding environs and thus enhance the public's awareness of the worshiping community and its impact on the neighborhood.

For moderately large-sized congregations such as Holy Ghost in Detroit and Eastbrook in Milwaukee, located as they are in crumbling urban neighborhoods where they focus their ministry, simply going to church on Sunday morning is a public statement. Worship is the mode of their most visible presence in the community. While people stream toward the church on foot or by car, traffic patterns, both vehicular and social, are affected each week.

At Holy Ghost, this is brought into sharp relief by the case of Luther, who gradually walked his way into the church. At first he came into the lobby in his self-assigned capacity of guardian and greeter; over time he began to stay for worship. Ultimately, he came fully into the church, coming to the faith. The deliverance the gospel brought to him lives on in his life in the neighborhood.

While more independent congregations and those with a shorter history seem to be able to develop their own unique missional identities within their neighborhoods fairly readily, congregations such as the IMPACT churches struggle with their 300-year-old Dutch Reformed, Atlantic seaboard heritage. In one church the worship planning team asks, "How can we make our worship missional?" They are asking what needs to be changed in light of the fact that they "no longer live in the Christian nation that our parents and grandparents took for granted." There is a formation process occurring as congregations discover new ways of understanding, acting on, and making relevant the historic faith confessions that have been part of their worship for three centuries. Even the difficulties mentioned above surrounding the efforts of the Rockaway Church are part of the shaping process of the congregation toward becoming more missional. Some newer, younger members have come into the congregation. Together with the conscious wrestling over styles, that has had an indirect shaping effect.

In each of these churches, worship is shaped uniquely by the congregation's cultural context. Worship at Holy Ghost is rooted deeply in the African-American tradition. The presence of immigrant communities in and around the Eastbrook Church is evident in the multiethnic, multilingual music of the worship. At West Yellowstone, worship blends popular styles in an informal atmosphere reminiscent of a television variety show, reflecting something of the culture of a small, isolated Western resort town: informal, open, relaxed. Of course, cultural forces are not the only ones deemed important. Church traditions, and the dialogue between those and a renewed sense of the calling of God discerned in the Scriptures, are shaping forces as well. The churches are led to questions like these: Can missional worship reflect and critique the surrounding culture at the same time? Can worship constitute prophetic resistance to the dominant culture while it utilizes the genres and modes of expression of that public culture? How can worship be expressed in incarnated ways at the same time as it maintains the proper critical distance that addresses local custom and popular choices with a call to conversion? How does the worship so shape the church that it keeps the church's sense of mission on course?

Hans Hoekendijk, a missionary leader of the mid-twentieth century, was remarking once about the emerging selfhood of the "younger churches" of the third world. Among several signs of what shows such a church to be authentic, he included this one: it composes and sings its own songs. On our visit to Eastbrook, the liturgy included a duet composed by one of the singers. It was not the first song she had composed and contributed to the church's worship. Music that comes thus from the heart of the congregation is frequently the most powerful expression of the way the gospel is good news there, in that particular congregation, for the gathered and for all others who live nearby.

Worship Permeates the Public Life of the Congregation

The folks at Transfiguration say: "People do not come to the Mass because of the music, but because of the impact the church has in the community." After our visits among these churches, we found ourselves less and less able to draw clear lines between public witness and worship in their experience. We began to see that their worship is public witness and their public witness is worship. If worship is a kind of public intervention, an acknowledgment of God's purposes, so also is the church's public witness. Worship motivates and permeates public action, for it is an encounter with the God who both calls his people out of the world and sends them into it.

In spite of the variety of public, creative, and often prophetic missional activities evidenced among the churches we visited, there was a singularity in the way they understood that their concern, involvement, and commitment to persevere in their missional engagements is motivated and sustained in their worship. And worship is never far from their public action.

Eastbrook deliberately located its worship center in a neighborhood neglected by many other churches and ministries. Some members of the congregation have moved into the neighborhood and have become involved in the programs of education, recreation, and racial reconciliation it has developed. Reconciliation is a central theme at Eastbrook, and worship is a reenactment and reinforcement of this theme, touching upon relationships within the worshiping community as well as on the way the church sees itself working in the broader community. In worship, this is done two ways: by celebrating diversity and by reinforcing solidarity. The conviction that "we are all sinners, reconciled to God and to one another" is celebrated and demonstrated weekly at Eastbrook's worship and continuously in the lives of the members in their relationships.

The understanding that "wherever our worship is located, that is where our ministry occurs" focuses Holy Ghost's outreach of "Christian community development" (to borrow a phrase from John Perkins), a complex of social ministries among the disadvantaged. That context shapes its message of hope and life-quality improvement as part of the good news of the gospel. "Deliverance" is the prominent theme. The message is clearly and directly communicated and demonstrated in both the public congregational worship and public activities in the community among families, the marginalized, and at-risk residents in the neighborhood.

At Spring Garden Church, the worship focus is shaped by, and shapes, the actions of the congregation in things like prayer walks, economic development projects, local evangelism, international mission teams, and social reconciliation. While not a church seeking a high profile as "political" or "activist," in 1997 Spring Garden found itself on the local Toronto news, quite apart from any intentional effort to get press there! In their province, a deadlock in negotiations between teachers and public school authorities prompted a strike. The church recognized that this would affect not only teachers and other school employees, but children and youth who would suddenly be out of school. Working parents would be forced to find child care on extremely short notice. A lot of chaos promised to follow as the strike began.

It is always the habit of Spring Garden to pray when things like this occur, and on this occasion it was no different. But as they prayed, they began to reason that if they were praying for the schools and the teachers and the students and their families, and if the God they were praying to was a real and living presence, then of course they must act in line with that confidence. Quickly, with primary initiatives from high school students and teachers within the congregation, they organized a Teachers' Strike Day School for as many children as they could accommodate. High schoolers became tutors to younger children, working parents were helped in the care of their out-of-school children — and the local news camera crew came to get some footage! The spontaneous initiative became a political act, born of their simple responsiveness to things they knew God cared about. These were simply their "lived prayers." Worship and public witness were joined at the hip.

Transfiguration's worship, centered as it is upon solidarity with the poorest of the poor, has direct connections with the forms that solidarity takes. Casa Bethsaida, a hospice for patients with AIDS; the Southside Community Mission which provides social services and meals for the homeless and immigrants; and the work of attorney Anne Pilsbury to advocate for immigrants all grows out of the constant pulse of the prayer of Charles de Foucauld, "Father, I abandon myself into your hands; do with me what you will. . . . I love you, Lord, and so need to give myself, to surrender myself into your hands, without reserve. . . ."

Of all the observations we made of the way worship and public witness are intertwined in the experience of these churches, two of the most poignant images are these:

At Rockridge United Methodist Church in Oakland, one of the Mission Covenant Groups moved in worship into the midst of their neighborhood in a vivid way. The group had concern for two things. First, they were artists who understood that art is an important expression of worship. A lot of what they did as a group grew out of that conviction. Second, they had concern for reconciliation among the people in the difficult neighborhood where they lived. The public act of worship they led included the invitation to their neighbors to carry rocks to the church property and name them as their fears, troubles, and burdens and then leave them behind. These rocks were permanently incorporated into the landscaping, resulting in an artistic display of liberation for all in the neighborhood to observe and ponder.

The connection between public action and worship would not seem to be apparent in the Boulder congregation. Social-activism types of ministries that include local political involvement, witness for social and economic justice, support of and participation on Christian Peacemaker Teams, the Victim-Offender Reconciliation Program, and Mennonite Voluntary Services are all part of the public face of Boulder Mennonite Church. The relationship between those ministries and the congregation's worship could easily be missed by the casual observer. But it is important to notice that prayer and singing are sometimes deliberately incorporated as part of the public actions. Even more interesting is the fact that work is currently being done to assemble a new collection of "songs appropriate for singing at public protests." In that effort the deep inner relationship between public witness and the worship of God is made obvious.

A rockscape and a book of protest worship songs are symbols paraded and erected, compiled and published to attest that the God and Father of Jesus Christ worshiped in ritual storytelling is the God of absolute care for the brokenness of the whole world. And this people called "church" is sent to bear witness to that!

> Our postmodern society has come to regard worship as the private, internal, and often arcane activity of religionists who retreat from the world to practice their mystical rites. By definition, however, the *ekklesia* is a public assembly, and its worship is its first form of mission. . . . The reality of God that is proclaimed in worship is to be announced to and for the entire world. The walls and windows of churches need to become transparent. (*Missional Church,* p. 243)

Pattern 6

Dependence on the Holy Spirit

WALTER C. HOBBS

"So that it may be made clear that this extraordinary power belongs to God and does not come from us."

(2 Cor. 4:7b)

Pattern: The missional community confesses its dependence upon the Holy Spirit, shown in particular in its practices of corporate prayer.

Words change. The meanings and pronunciations and spelling of words, even the contexts in which words are used, are always in flux. The English word *bankruptcy* is an example. In an earlier day, a craftsman who could not pay his debts stood in danger of watching his creditors smash his workbench to smithereens (another witless practice in the sorry history of getting even, about as sensible as debtor's prison). He was said to have been bankrupted — *benc* [Old English] *ruptura* [Latin]. Today, however, a person who cannot pay his or her debts may seek legal protection against creditors by filing *for* bankruptcy. The workbench still gets smashed, so to speak, but the debtor has a bit more say in the process.

Many words that had been part of the common vocabulary in pre-Enlightenment days, such as *knight* and *squire*, either have disappeared from everyday speech or have been confined to very specific areas of modern life. Religion has retained a few of these terms, but much of their significance has been diluted or nullified over time. A free modern citizenry, jealous of its individual liberties and democratic governance, lacks the working context in which to appreciate earlier understandings of such concepts as lord, sovereign and subject, master and servant, worship. And prayer.

Prayer has been especially altered over the past five hundred years. It once meant a carefully worded request made by an individual or individuals of low social station to a more powerful figure. Sometimes it took the form of a legal process; sometimes it was less structured. But the stakes were always high. Moreover, the pray-er was acutely aware that he or she had no claim of right in the matter. The grant of the request lay wholly in the discretion of the one to whom it had been brought. The pray-er was completely dependent upon the goodwill and the might of the one to whom the plea was addressed. Consequently, such "prayer" was serious business. A person did not take for granted the opportunity to petition the superior power. Nor was that opportunity exercised lightly when it materialized.

It is probable that many twenty-first-century westerners who consider themselves Christian would hold that contemporary religious prayer still carries the earlier connotations of the word: serious, carefully framed petitions brought by needy, powerless people to the all-powerful God of the universe for disposition as God sees fit. It is not probable, however, that many local congregations reflect such views in their corporate behavior. Prayer is more often than not either privatized or ceremonialized — or neglected. It is commonly thought to serve either as "a port in the storm" or as a routinized religious exercise. Seldom is prayer, especially corporate prayer, born of a sense of abject dependence upon the God of the universe for the determination of congregational ministry.

Yet prayer is central to the missiological enterprise. The prospects for a congregation that spends little time together in prayer are stark. Consider Paul's comments in 2 Corinthians 4:6-11 (as paraphrased in Eugene H. Peterson's *The Message* [Colorado Springs: NavPress, 1995]):

> God said, "Light up the darkness!" and our lives filled up with
> light as we saw and understood God in the face of Christ, all

bright and beautiful. If you only look at us, you might well miss the brightness. We carry this precious Message around in the unadorned clay pots of our ordinary lives. That's to prevent anyone from confusing God's incomparable power with us.

As it is, there's not much chance of that. You know for yourselves that we're not much to look at.

We've been surrounded and battered by troubles, but we're not demoralized. We're not sure what to do, but we know that God knows what to do. We've been spiritually terrorized, but God hasn't left our side. We've been thrown down, but we haven't broken. What they did to Jesus, they do to us — trial and torture, mockery and murder. What Jesus did among them, he does in us — he lives! Our lives are at constant risk for Jesus' sake, which makes Jesus' life all the more evident in us.

Empty clay jars simply do not fare well in such an environment as Paul describes here. A people sent on *missio dei* (the mission of God) who do not constantly pray are bound to lurch along in confusion and pain. Trouble will surely batter them; indecision will plague them; evil will terrorize them.

Under such assaults, clay jars break easily, save for the sustaining life of Christ that fills them. The early churches knew this well (Acts 21:5), and just in case they might forget it they were often reminded by the apostles (see 1 Thess. 5:17, for example). Prayer was essential to the people of God in their mission of carrying Good News to the nations.

It still is. The missional church is incapable of fulfilling its call, save for guidance from the Spirit of God and for the Spirit's empowerment of the church's witness to that reality.

Dependence on the Holy Spirit

The reasons are not difficult to discern. To be the church, the Body of Christ, is to be completely dependent upon the Spirit's intimate relationship with the Father (Rom. 8:26-28). It is by engagement with the Spirit that those who follow Jesus find the Father's perfect will performed in them. Stated differently, prayer is quintessentially a Trinitarian affirmation. To "pray God's blessing" (or power or presence or any other demonstration of God's grace) upon a congregation's missional efforts is to presume the Spirit's active involvement in the life and work of the Body of Christ. Provision of material means, protection from the powers of darkness, growth in unconditional love extended even to enemies, inexplicable peace when everything appears to be in disarray, hope which confidently envisions the reign of God both present and future, sheer courage and unmitigated joy in the face of severe testing — all such resources are unstintingly provided to people who constantly seek their God. Prayer is essential to faithfulness in the missional venture.

One is not surprised, therefore, to find that, unlike the typical church in contemporary North America, congregations whose intent is to be missional in character are enthusiastic about prayer. They go about it in different ways, and their focus is shaped by their distinctive circumstances. Within their diversity, however, prayer is a common feature of each church's response to the call to be his witnesses.

Consider Boulder Mennonite Church. Members of the congregation wanted to sponsor an exhibit called "Peace Factory," but to do it as it ought to be done would be expensive. This church, however, recognizes that the God on whom their existence as a congregation depends is the God who owns every animal of the forest, the cattle on a thousand hills, and all the creatures of the field (Ps. 50:10-11). In *missio dei,* therefore, expense is simply not an issue! "Do it," the church council told the project team. "If God favors it, the money will be there."

The availability of material resources, however, was at times the lesser of their concerns. Elsewhere in this book we have written of Boulder Mennonite's response to the riots on the hill. A genuine risk of suffering physical violence accompanied the commitment of people in the congregation to mingle among the police and the rioters in an effort to defuse the hostilities by speaking peace. Nonetheless, once more they entrusted their "clay jars" to God to use as he saw fit. They prayed. Then they walked and talked calmly, persuasively — and safely — through the day.

Rockridge United Methodist Church can tell a different story about a problem that, it turned out, moved them from peril to opportunity. At Rockridge, there are close bonds among participants in the various Mission Covenant Groups. One of these groups had joined forces with a nearby sister congregation to become involved in the lives of children attending a neighborhood inner-city school. A member of that group, a master teacher in the California public system, told the others that he was considering a move from his well-supported suburban school to that inner-city location. Doing so would give the MCG additional legitimacy in their attempts to be of service there. However, it was not clear that the principal would welcome him should he apply, and he would certainly incur a substantial salary decrease were the move to take place. So he needed to be sure he was pursuing God's will in the matter. Over several months the group prayed with and for their brother, asking the Spirit to show them what ought to be done.

He did make the change. But almost immediately thereafter, the teachers' union in his new district called their members out on strike! The Mission Covenant Group had continued to pray with their friend concerning his new work environment and their collective ministry to the school. As they prayed, the realization took root that the Lord intended them to make up their brother's salary loss occasioned by the strike. Until it was over, therefore, they kept him financially secure.

The IMPACT churches faced persistent problems that at any time could disrupt their hopes for missional transformation. Since they had chosen to embark upon a significant and intentional process that the majority of their sister churches had chosen to forgo, they were "on their own." There was stiff resistance from among some in their ecclesial tradition. Other obstacles to missional transformation added to the daunting nature of their journey. In some participating congregations, material resources were scanty. In one congregation, two key leaders in the process died unexpectedly within months of each other. Mindsets often appeared impossible to change. It seemed at times they were taking one step forward and two back. In the midst of this, pastors covenanted to meet together many hours each month, month after month. As they puzzled through new insights, they prayed for one another in their respective difficulties. As the elders held up Moses' arms so that the battle would be successful, pastors and other leaders gathered frequently to hold up one another's arms. In this covenanted relationship, leaders of these congregations together saw clearly that in this particular project they were wholly, unarguably, completely dependent upon the Spirit of God to carry them through. Not to pray was not an option. Said one of the participants, "People are experiencing the benefits of praying together and meeting together instead of struggling alone."

It was a key discovery for these churches that over the years they had lost the practice of depending upon the leading of the Holy Spirit. As one congregation phrased it (for themselves), "We have done a good job dealing with various tangible aspects of church life such as facilities and funding, but we are uncomfortable and inexperienced in dealing with the tough issue of being led by the Spirit in present times." That recognition played a major role in the decision of these fellowships to discern God's call by recovering some of the ancient yet critical exercises of the faithful, among them convening for the express purpose of approaching their God in prayer in order to hear God's voice.

Persisting in Prayer

The phrase "Holy Ghost" is not a mere label to signify the Detroit congregation's religious identity. The church called the Holy Ghost Full Gospel Baptist Church uses every word in the name intentionally, and they look to the Spirit of God for continuing power to live up to it. Every Friday night, members of the congregation gather in circles to pray about the activities planned for the upcoming Sunday. They do not take for granted that worship which pleases the Father, learning that changes lives, and fellowship that knits many members into one Body, will simply "happen." Such outcomes take place only when the Holy Ghost comes upon the people *in power* — one can hear the resounding phrase ring out. As Sunday passes and another week begins, 40 to 50 people gather again on Monday morning, and Tuesday and Wednesday and Thursday as well, to bathe each day in prayer. There is no doubt among these people that being in close touch with the God in whom they live and move and have their being is an absolute necessity.

In Brooklyn, the Roman Catholic parish, Transfiguration, joins its time of prayer to a corporate meal and study. Every Saturday morning, people committed to the parish ministry of "serving the poorest of the poor" join in an hour of silent adoration, then share a meal together and study the Word. Father Bryan marvels at the outcome: "It's just uncanny; the money's always there."

Uncanny? Perhaps not. Transfiguration has adopted as its "prayer of surrender" a statement known as "Brother Charles's Prayer of Abandonment":

> Father, I abandon myself into your hands; do with me what you will. Whatever you may do, I thank you; I am ready for all, I accept all. Let only your will be done in me, and in all your creatures. I wish no more than this, O Lord. Into your hands I commend my soul; I offer it to you with all the love of my heart, for I love you, Lord, and so need to give myself, to surrender myself into your hands, without reserve and with boundless confidence, for you are my Father.

One of the Transfiguration parishioners said to us, "Attempting this prayer is an ongoing challenge for us." Undoubtedly his emphasis was on the word *challenge*. But in truth it is the ongoing-ness of that prayer that distinguishes this parish. Their abandonment to the will of God — "with boundless confidence" — is transparent. When the parish priest, Father Karvelis, was asked what Bible passage best describes Transfiguration he pointed to Jesus' sending of the Seventy (Luke 12) and of the Twelve (Mark 6). "We don't have programs. It's just showing love, proclaiming the gospel. St. Francis [of Assisi] said, 'Trust that God is good.' No kidding! Trust him. Really!"

West Yellowstone members "tilled the soil" with prayer, waiting for God to send the pastoral team that has since led the missional transformation of the church. The lesson has not been forgotten: prayer is still fundamental to their ecclesial practice.

In Toronto, members of the Spring Garden congregation engage in prayer walks: they stroll the streets of their urban neighborhood, praying with particularity for the people there who need to meet the Master — residents, business owners, customers, even tourists. Like Transfiguration Parish in Brooklyn, Spring Garden never lacks the material resources to do whatever they sense at any given time they have been called to do. Their intent is to serve others in the imaginative ways God has gifted them to do, and it seems not to occur to them that they might run short of anything they need to obey.

Eastbrook Church runs on prayer. Mondays through Fridays, people gather every morning at 6:00. First they read a passage of Scripture, then as a group they pray about whatever is on their minds. After 20 to

25 minutes of collective prayer, they break into circles of three to five persons, and they pray for people who on the previous Sunday have filled out "praise and request" forms for the purpose. On the fifth Wednesday of a month, the weekly evening Bible study is replaced by a time of prayer for ministries beyond the church, both local to the Milwaukee area and elsewhere. On the second Saturday morning of each month, people gather to pray from 6:30 to 8:00, following which they have breakfast together and hear from someone for whom they've been praying regarding what God has been doing in his or her life. Twice each year, in the spring and in the fall, all organized programs of ministry are technically suspended. Opportunity is provided to all members to gather to pray with one another Monday through Friday from 6:00 to 7:00 a.m., from 12:00 to 1:00 p.m., and from 6:30 to 8:00 p.m. Not every ministry group in the congregation participates (several "kinship groups" decline to meet with the Body on their scheduled nights), but the message nonetheless is stated unambiguously: "Eastbrook prays." Equally unambiguous is the typical opening prayer at the start of a worship service: "Lord, much as we want to worship you, this isn't something we are able to do on our own. Without the Spirit of God working in us and through us and among us, nothing of any value will take place here today. We are nothing without you. Work in us we pray, so that we can worship you!"

In a world where even small groups find it difficult to get together regularly with everyone showing up, most congregations consider the practice of corporate, collective prayer virtually impossible. And in an individualized, privatized culture, the knee-jerk response is often "So what? Where does it say we must?"

Missional transformation, however, is countercultural to the core. People who want to be serious about "the *church* as the hermeneutic of the gospel" will have to grapple with the demands of the corporate life for their own lives as individuals. The many individual members comprise one Body, an *ekklesia*, a local assembly of God's people. When the Second Person of the Trinity assumed a human body, he suffered all the frailties and vulnerabilities visited on the rest of humanity. It was unthinkable to him not to be in constant communication with the Father. For him prayer was not an onerous duty, not even a useful discipline to be observed. It was his lifeline in a world flooded with death.

The Body of Christ today is no less frail, no less vulnerable, no less afloat in a sea of death than was Jesus Christ two millennia ago. But the Spirit gives life! So "be joyful always; pray continually; give thanks in all circumstances, for this is God's will for you in Christ Jesus. Do not put out the Spirit's fire" (1 Thess. 5:16-19).

> To pray "your will be done" is to submit ourselves to God, to be open to God's testing and to God's initiatives. Prayer is not about getting what we want — the fulfillment of our will; it is about learning what God wants — the bending of our will to God's will. (*Missional Church,* pp. 157-58)

Pointing Toward the Reign of God

DARRELL L. GUDER

"For this slight momentary affliction is preparing us for an eternal weight of glory beyond all measure, because we look not at what can be seen but at what cannot be seen; for what can be seen is temporary, but what cannot be seen is eternal."
(2 Cor. 4:17-18)

Pattern: The missional church understands its calling as witness to the gospel of the in-breaking reign of God and strives to be an instrument, agent, and sign of that reign. As it makes its witness through its identity, activity, and communication, it is aware of the provisional character of all that it is and does. It points toward the reign of God which God will certainly bring about, but knows that its own response is incomplete and that its own conversion is a continuing necessity.

A pastor of one of the IMPACT congregations in New Jersey described the process of missional change that they have been experiencing with these words:

We are beginning to see the purpose of the community as cultivating a people of a contrasting lifestyle. To see the kingdom community at the center, and one's own identity as a kingdom person, that's a 180-degree change. Most people here can accept this in theory, but many would still say, "This doesn't sound like normal American life to me."

This pastor's reference to "kingdom community" accents a theme that has emerged as central to our understanding of the missional church. The consensus has grown and taken root that this theme is crucial to the church's vocation now. A great deal of scholarly work in the New Testament throughout the twentieth century supports this conviction. The reign, or kingdom, of God was the central theme of Jesus' preaching, as the Synoptic Gospels make plain. But it is a theme that is strangely absent from the missionary message of the Western churches. This has been true for a very long time. Many dilutions and distortions of Jesus' message of the kingdom have grown up. The most obvious distortion was the idea that Christianized Western civilization from Constantine onward was, in fact, God's kingdom on earth. The linkage between church and state, throne and altar, symbolized this. The church of Christendom, which saw itself as God's kingdom on earth, had virtually no sense of its missionary vocation.

That older distortion has been replaced by more recent versions. Sometimes Christians understand the reign of God as a particular program of social and economic justice, which we are to build as God's agents. Sometimes it is interpreted in a private and individualistic way: God's rule is a matter of Jesus' lordship in the personal life of the Christian. Sometimes it is dealt with solely as a matter of the future: God's kingdom is what Christ will inaugurate at the Second Coming. The challenge before us was twofold: to attempt definitions of how the criterion of witness to God's reign might in fact be present and work in a congregation, and then to discern that happening in the congregations we visited.

The Reign of God as a Missional Challenge

The contemporary work of biblical scholars is challenging us to rediscover the centrality and the mystery of the reign of God at the heart of the gospel. The mission of the apostolic church clearly centers on the proclamation and demonstration of the in-breaking reign of God. This conviction was influential in the study which generated *Missional Church* (see especially chapters 4-6 there). It carried forward into the present research project, finding its expression in the criteria that guided both our choice of churches to investigate and the inquiry process we adopted. We said that one of the hallmarks of a missional congregation would be its recognition that the church itself is an incomplete expression of the reign of God. We agreed that, in such congregations, there would be a widely held perception that this church was moving toward a more faithfully lived life under the reign of God. One evidence that missional transformation is happening would be the awareness that the church is as yet a flawed witness to the kingdom of God. It would be intentionally open to its own reformation as it sought to be more faithful in its witness. It would constantly give a critique of its own vision based on its scriptural formation and discipling. It would be willing to be measured against the biblical definition of God's reign. It would be wary of the culturally established standards of success that might be equated with "kingdom faithfulness." It would signal a genuine sense of openness to its own continuing conversion. It would be willing to change as it sensed God leading it toward such decisions. In discernible ways, such a congregation would live its life and make its decisions in response to what is yet to come.

After struggling with these issues within our team and seeking to pursue them in our congregational analyses, we are more persuaded than ever that concrete witness to the present and coming reign of God is essential to missional faithfulness. But we are also profoundly conscious of the difficulties surrounding this pattern. We all are more shaped by our Christendom legacy than we are prepared to admit. Without always knowing that we are doing so, we go along with the deeply rooted assumptions we inherit. Some really believe that they know what the kingdom of God is like, and it is suspiciously close to the kinds of churches they are or want to be. We often compromise with the pressures of our social context as they try to shape us. We blunt the cutting edge of the claim that Jesus is Lord in myriad ways, while making that faith confession as sincerely as we can.

Our investigations have helped us to discern indications of this transformative spiritual process in a church. But since this is clearly the sovereign work of God, we are now much more modest in our claims and analyses than we were when we set out. We have not discovered a guaranteed method to initiate "kingdom of God awareness" in a congregation. There are, we believe, some helpful ways to look for and understand how this transformation to missional calling may be taking place.

Conviction and Modesty: The Missional Church's Self-Understanding

The IMPACT churches are convinced that they are on a journey, in the wilderness, on a pilgrimage, moving toward the Promised Land. They know that they are not the church envisioned in the New Testament, but they want to discover its defining meaning for their vocation today. They readily admit that they don't know what the biblical kingdom of God looks like, but they want to find out and are on the path of exploration and often discovery. Much of the energy that motivates them to continue this exploration is what they have already discovered and how much more they want to find. But they are very candid about themselves: "When we started this process we were in a confused state, and today we are in a confused state." They have moved, gone through painful passages, discovered much, and have not arrived. They are still struggling, but they are struggling with transformation itself. They reported on this process to their Synod:

> We have begun to recognize how insidiously the culture has entwined itself in our belief systems, ecclesial understanding, and our polity. . . . We have experienced an emerging spiritual awakening through IMPACT Bible studies, continued adult education, congregational gatherings, small groups, worship, and IMPACT teams. We have begun to return to the reformed understanding: by grace alone, by faith alone, and by Scripture alone. . . . We have begun to rethink how we "evaluate" the work of the church. No longer does success equal large attendance, breadth of programming, and big budgets. We take fewer offerings and count fewer noses. Instead we ask whether God was present and how Jesus and the Holy Spirit moved us during our time together.

A comparable modesty, coupled with determination, can be experienced at Boulder Mennonite Church. One member said, "This church has a lot of flaws, but we keep loving each other and hope to be getting more like Christ." Speaking for virtually all of the churches, one person said, "A real indicator of a missional church might be that it thinks that the kingdom of God hasn't arrived yet and may be in the process of coming."

The theme of the reign of God is evidenced at Rockridge in their vision statement and their worship music. They are deeply aware of their need to be shaped by God's word; they desire to change and be changed. They are honest and forthright about the problem of pride. They have, after all, made a radical commitment to the Mission Covenant Groups, but now have to deal with the difficulties created by such commitments. What, they ask themselves, does it mean for their relationship to brothers and sisters who don't share their commitments but want to be part of the church? They have a radical vision, which could be defined as a vision of the lordship of Christ, and yet they are puzzled about how to get there and still be caring, open, and inviting to those who don't agree with them. Their modesty with regard to the reign of Christ has been shaped by a discovery: decisions don't result in the comfort of "having arrived" but create their own new discontinuities and challenges.

In a church as outwardly "successful" as First Presbyterian, Bellevue, the question of response to the reign of Christ is a challenge for the pastoral leadership. The senior pastor candidly expressed his own sense of their incompleteness over against their biblical calling. He knows that this emphasis is not the priority of many members. He is grappling with the question seriously and wants to probe further. He wonders if their gift of administration, of careful and effective planning and management, tends to resolve the problem by centering on activism. There is, among many of the leaders, a sense of congregational journey, but it can easily be confused or obscured with their versions of progress and the confidence of many that they ought to be able to come up with a plan that works. In their struggle, they represent the tensions facing North American Christians who want to respond wholeheartedly to the claims of the reign of Christ and often confuse those claims with institutional success.

The Holy Ghost congregation, with its Pentecostal formation, links its understanding and practice of the reign of Christ with the work of the Spirit. They see themselves as part of the global movement of the Spirit. They testify that the Spirit is surprising them, is not under their control, and is doing something bigger that includes them. Their mission in their neighborhood is far from completed, and never will be. They always have cause to learn obedience and holiness. The young people of the congregation wrote a letter to Bishop Corletta Vaughn saying that they did not feel that they were truly incorporated into the life and decision making of the church. They wanted a place to be mentored and to be a part of the congregation's mission. She responded openly with a confession, an act of repentance toward them, and an expression of her willingness to work with them.

Openness and the need to change are strong emphases at Spring Garden Church. They are profoundly aware of their human sinfulness and frailties, knowing that in spite of that, they are part of God's presence and work in that city. They describe themselves as a community of wounded people being healed, fully aware of their incompleteness. The first impression they give is of their awareness that they are a broken people in a broken world, but they know that God is at work.

Eastbrook's preaching also emphasizes human sinfulness and the need for grace. The congregation is told that they should not judge others, as flawed as they themselves are. They are modest in comparing themselves to other communities. They stress forgiveness precisely because they are flawed and incomplete. They understand that relationships are always in formation and never finished, so they expect continual growth and healing. The pastor demonstrates this himself as a mixture of certainty, confidence, and genuine humility. The older members speak openly about "how far he has come." They recognize his deep awareness of imperfection and are even a little puzzled that anyone wants to investigate what is happening in their community. They don't think that they have come very far as a church.

The West Yellowstone Church is in a process of rapid growth and development, which has been encouraged by the openness and modesty of its older generation. Before the present pastor came, they prayed consciously for the growth and change of the church. They knew that it would have to become something different from what they were used to and cherished. But they wanted that to happen, and intentionally "gave the church" to its next generation to make the changes and moves that would be discerned as necessary. It happened not without loss and pain, however, especially as they moved away from the familiar forms of worship. That spirit of openness has been a positive factor in the church's present spiritual pilgrimage.

The priest at Transfiguration Church has a poster on the wall with the motto, "Happiness is found along the way and not at the end of the road." Movement and open-endedness are intentional disciplines of this community. They are facing a hard passage of change as their priest's tenure moves toward conclusion after decades of inspired leadership. But they have learned through the weekly disciplines of the fraternities to address the issues of their own incompleteness and to face the renewal and correction they need.

There is, we think, a provocative insight to be gained in regard to missional awareness of the in-breaking reign of God. All of these churches appear, in varying degrees, to know that their definitions and assumptions about the lordship of Christ in their midst are too small. They are moving beyond the reductionism of the Christendom legacy and opening themselves up to the prospect that God might answer the prayer, "thy kingdom come," in surprising ways. They are not overly confident that they know the shape of the kingdom, but they are earnestly committed to their own formation to be its witnesses.

Nevertheless: Discerning Kingdom Hope

To be sure, at Transfiguration Parish, one seldom hears the specific language of the reign of God. But the presence and rule of Christ is the constant theme underlying the life of the church and infusing its liturgy. Centered on the Eucharist as the celebration of the real presence of Christ, the congregation constantly expresses its desire to submit to him, to follow him, and to minister as he ministered. In the fraternities, a prayer of surrender is prayed weekly, expressing corporate submission to the lordship of Christ. The fraternities' focus upon the adoration of Christ in the Eucharist, part of the charismatic legacy of Brother Charles de Foucauld, is a concrete expression of submission to Christ's powerful presence and lordship.

The preaching of the kingdom of God forms the intentional center of the Boulder Mennonite Church. The biblical language of God's reign is an essential dimension of their formation. They describe themselves as a community seeking to live now the values of the reign of God, pointing the way toward God's purposes for all the world. They understand their engagement in public witness as a way of signaling the coming reign of God.

To the Reformed congregations of the IMPACT project, the theme of God's reign has become a defining emphasis. They also speak of the household of God and the Body of Christ, and link these biblical themes together as they try to work out their implications. As they have sought to discern their future vision, this central biblical emphasis has asserted itself so that they now have to use the language of the reign of God to define their purpose. They say, "We are changing completely. And that changing stems from the growing vision of our church as a kingdom people — a people meant to manifest the kingdom of God on earth — to the extent that we can allow the Holy Spirit to show and guide us."

They are learning to say about themselves that they exist to be a foretaste of the reign of God, against all appearances and over constant resistance.

> We have looked into the face of the death of our congregations as we have known them, and still find hope. It is the hope of the transformation of persons to a deeper understanding and relationship with God, and the hope of the promises of God for the church: "a living, breathing body, made up of many, guided by the one head, Jesus, who is the Christ." We are living into the hope of being the very Kingdom of God itself in our hurting and broken world.

The language of the reign of God is not an obvious aspect of the community life of the Holy Ghost Church or the Spring Garden Church. But at Holy Ghost, there is constant emphasis upon the powerful way in which Christ works in their lives. They stress personal and communal holiness to honor Christ, and their desire to be obedient to the Word of God with mutual accountability. The theme of deliverance, which is strong in this community, is a demonstration of the lordship of Christ at work. At Spring Garden, they see themselves as called and equipped to be Christ's presence in the city, and they frequently express their confidence in Christ's ultimate victory. They see their confidence in Christ as a testimony to his lordship, even though kingdom language is not current.

While being careful not to claim too much, we can state that there are discernible signs of kingdom hope at work in these churches. Candor about their incompleteness need not and should not conceal joy at the hopeful signs of God's converting work, going on in both subtle and obvious ways. Discerning these signs of God's work only compounds the gift and importance of the kingdom hope that God's Spirit gives as essential equipping for the passage of continuing conversion.

Local Witness to Global Reign

The confession that God's reign is breaking in takes on concrete form in a congregation's witness to the global reign of God. There are discernible signs of God's global reign shaping the life and witness of these congregations. Kingdom awareness expresses itself in the ways a community senses and practices its connectedness to the church beyond its boundaries. Some of the congregations under review are parts of denominations that relate parishes to larger structures. There are also defined ecumenical relationships and commitments that are part of denominational identity. Our interest here is not simply a question of denominational connections or institutional ecumenism. The real issue is the linkage between missional renewal and our essential relatedness to the global and multicultural church. We sense that the vision of the missional church as a witness to God's reign over all the world must lead to different institutional strategies, to new ways of connecting and interacting, to movement beyond existing patterns.

Such movement cannot be programmed or turned into strategies, but it is apparently happening in a great diversity of emerging networks and shared forms of ministry. The pattern of modest expectation of the reign of God includes, we suggest, a concrete sense of God's mysterious rule at work around the world and across history. Through that work, God is linking particular communities to each other so that they can be more faithful in their witness. We were interested in the ways in which missional transformation might be traced in the connectedness of these congregations.

For a Roman Catholic parish, the connectedness is obvious. Transfiguration participates in diocesan activities, although not without resistance. They enjoy sharing about their parish life with others. The diocese assists them with funding for their AIDS hospice. Their distinctiveness makes them a well-known church. Seminaries send students there to learn more about its ministries and character. In another, less obvious sense, the congregation is linked with churches in other countries because of the high percentage of immigrants in its membership. As a church dominated by Hispanic culture, it is connected across the boundaries of the United States and has, without having to try to do so, a real sense of the global nature of the church. The multicultural character of God's reign is more a given than an intentional emphasis of this unusual church.

At the other end of the cultural spectrum, First Presbyterian Church of Bellevue works intentionally to develop a sense of the connected church among its members. The denominational connection, although taken seriously, is probably not as significant here as are the church's mission partnerships. The congregation has started such partnerships with sister churches in Russia and Central America. They have taken these relationships seriously, prepare carefully for their travel and visitations, and try to be responsible in their follow-through. (The "mission trip" has become a favorite form of missional education in prosperous churches of the West. There is no denying its value, although questions must be raised about the approach. There is the obvious question of wealth: rich Christians generally visit poor Christians. How significant are the work projects that are often the programs of such ventures? What do the demands of hospitality and hosting require of partner churches, and how sensitive are the visitors to those demands? From the perspective of missional transformation, how does a North American congregation engage in cross-cultural mission in such a way that its own missionary vocation, where it is, becomes clearer and more defined?)

At another level, the pastoral leadership at Bellevue has developed a regional network with congregations in their area to address the challenges of their neighborhoods. This network crosses denominational lines and links the church with congregations from diverse traditions. Bellevue's pastors have been criticized from within their denomination for having partnerships with non-mainline churches, but they find this to be an important way to broaden the missional vision of their congregation.

Denominational linkages are also a part of the structure in which the Rockridge Church lives. Their relationships are troubled, however, by their dissent from some of the policies endorsed by their United Methodist district. Early on, they experienced their denomination as a mixed blessing, although their superintendent has helped them resolve conflicts. They have a "sister church" in San Francisco and ongoing links with the Church of the Savior in Washington, D.C. Long-term and short-term international links eventually led to the creation of an "Ends of the Earth" Mission Covenant Group that focused on supporting boundary crossing, both local and international.

For the West Yellowstone Church, denominational linkages are important, if only because they are located in an isolated area. Both pastors are active in denominational work all the way up to the national level. They also are related to a renewal network of Presbyterian churches and have taken strong leadership in the area of small church ministries. Their members benefit from being drawn into such experiences with other congregations. Their young people take mission trips and are helped by the church to discover the global nature of the church.

Both denominational and local linkages are important for the Boulder Church. The Mennonite network draws members and pastors beyond the boundaries of the congregation as they work in boards and committees. In Boulder, they work together with many churches of many traditions in running a Victim-Offender Reconciliation Program.

The IMPACT congregations are linked in the Reformed Church in America, which entails the normal requirements and struggles of connectional duties. In fact, the pastors of these congregations have been called upon to provide important leadership at the denominational level. But at this stage, their most important experience of the connectedness of the church is the relationship they are building with each other. In spite of all that they hold in common, the more they work on their network, the more they discover that missional connectedness is a hard discipline and a constant challenge.

This is especially true in North America, where the entrepreneurial system fosters congregational independence. Church members tend to feel that they "own" their churches and often struggle with the claim that they are called to be Christ's people. The connectedness that truly fosters missional transformation teaches members that God is calling and sending a vast diversity of communities to service. What they have in common is their calling, their message, and their hope. They can discover through the eyes of others that they are more captive to their culture than they knew. They can also be encouraged by the demonstration of God's rule at work in the multicultural church around the world.

There is a distinctive kind of connectedness at work in the Holy Ghost congregation. Through Bishop Vaughn, they are linked to the International Communion of Charismatic Churches, connecting them with congregations and ministries around the world, especially in Africa. Bishop Vaughn's ordination as a bishop derives from that communion. She has initiated some 60 ministries in her role as a bishop. With her, the congregation is consciously part of a worldwide network of charismatic churches, which often means that they are traveling elsewhere or entertaining guests from around the world. They have a vibrant sense of the connected, global church, not so much as a denomination (although they are loosely tied to the National Baptist Convention), but as a dynamic work of the Spirit.

Many visitors from other churches seek out Eastbrook Church. Some are evangelized in the process. The pastor is closely connected to many other pastors and churches, ranging from African-American storefront churches to mainline and Roman Catholic congregations. The congregation's connections are, however, largely carried out by the pastoral leaders, who are concerned about the welfare of these linked churches and keep informed about what is going on. When Eastbrook has visitors from other churches present, they are likely to pray for the churches represented by their visitors and to send them back with greetings and encouragement. Their understanding of connectedness is practiced as partnership and mutual encouragement. There are no denominational ties to work with.

Similarly, formal ties to the Canadian Baptist Church are insignificant for Spring Garden. They value their organic ties to local ministries in Toronto, including their networks with Roman Catholics and Pentecostals, with whom they cooperate in various ministries. The congregation has its own network of international connections, sends many missionaries abroad, and experiences constant exchange with ministries beyond their boundaries. Their membership includes many internationals from metropolitan Toronto.

When we surveyed the congregations, asking about their sense of their witness to the reign of God, we discovered that missional formation is happening through the experience of tension, struggle with change, dealing with resistance, and exciting breakthroughs into new understandings of vocation. There is a keen awareness of who they are, what they believe God wants them to become, and what remains to be discovered and risked. In diverse ways, they would affirm that "this slight momentary affliction is preparing us for an eternal weight of glory beyond all measure." They do not see their institutional structures, their programs, or their present levels of development as ends in themselves, although the temptation is never far away to do so. They are striving to focus on "what cannot be seen" in a cultural context that places enormous value in what can be seen. They are confident that God will complete the good work begun in them, although sometimes they would like to set the schedule. With all the struggles of these congregations, this awareness of incompleteness, this knowledge of the need to change, and this openness to growth are modest but compelling evidence that transformation is taking place.

> In summary, the church in mission may be characterized as the sign of Messiah's coming. Our being, doing, and speaking are signs that his coming is "already" and "not yet." He is here already or the signs would not be present. He is coming still or the signs would not be muted. Broken though they may be, the signs persist in the world by the Spirit's insistence, and they spell hope for the renewal of the human community in the final reconciliation of all things to God through the Lord, Christ. In this respect, the church is the preview community, the foretaste and harbinger of the coming reign of God. (*Missional Church*, p. 108)

Pattern 8

Missional Authority

JEFF VAN KOOTEN AND LOIS BARRETT

"For we do not preach ourselves, but Jesus Christ as Lord, and ourselves as your servants for Jesus' sake."

(2 Cor. 4:5)

Pattern: The Holy Spirit gives the missional church a community of persons who, in a variety of ways and with a diversity of functional roles and titles, together practice the missional authority that cultivates within the community the discernment of missional vocation and is intentional about the practices that embed that vocation in the community's life.

When our team first identified indicators of the missional character of a congregation, missional authority was not one of them. Perhaps we took for granted issues of authority or leadership. Yet when we visited the congregations in our sample, we discovered some particular patterns regarding authority. So when we gathered as a team to assess and categorize our findings, we realized that missional authority needed to be included in our list of patterns of what it means to be on the journey toward missional transformation.

The chasm between the church's understanding of authority and that of the dominant culture is much wider than we realized. A church conditioned by Christendom is often tempted to begin with the concept of authority as defined by culture and then seeks to find whether the church has that kind of authority. The result is a church whose authority is relegated to individual and private spheres.

We found that the business-related books on "leadership" were not adequate to describe the leaders of the congregations in our sample. Nor did we find helpful the Enlightenment idea of authority granted by consent of the governed — a concept usually applied to nonprofit organizations in the dominant culture. We sensed that missional leaders did not necessarily lead through their "office." There was not just one leader. Nor was everybody a "leader." We needed a more biblically based understanding of authority in order to sense the pattern of missional authority in these churches.

Authority Comes from God

Throughout the Bible, the ultimate authority comes from God. Exodus 15, one of the earliest parts of the Bible to be put into writing, celebrates God's rule: "The Lord will reign forever and ever" (v. 18). On through the Book of Revelation, the Bible proclaims God's reign: "The kingdom of the world has become the kingdom of our Lord and of his Messiah, and he will reign forever and ever" (11:15).

Through the anointing of prophets, priests, and kings in the Old Testament and the laying on of hands in the early church, God gave authority to human beings to govern the people of God. But God's Spirit has brought the church into being, and the church remains God's. This goes counter to the understanding of the dominant culture in the West, where organizations and governments are brought into being by a contract between members or citizens. Nonprofit associations (the actual legal status of the church in the United States and Canada) are assumed to be "owned" by, and to function for the benefit of, the members and their goals. But the church is God's. Jesus Christ is the head of the church by God's authority, not because church members voted him in. In the Gospels, Jesus speaks and acts as one with authority — authority given by God.

The Roman centurion who has faith that Jesus will heal his slave understands the kind of authority that Jesus has:

"But only speak the word, and let my servant be healed. For I also am a man set under authority, with soldiers under me; and I say to one, 'Go,' and he goes, and to another, 'Come,' and he comes, and to my slave, 'Do this,' and the slave does it."

When Jesus heard this, he was amazed at him, and turning to the crowd that followed him, he said, "I tell you, not even in Israel have I found such faith." (Luke 7:7b-9)

Jesus' authority comes from God, and the church's authority comes from Jesus, who sent out the Twelve and "gave them authority over unclean spirits, to cast them out, and to cure every disease and every sickness" (Matt. 10:1) and commissions his disciples with the words, "All authority in heaven and on earth has been given to me" (Matt. 28:18).

But Jesus' authority is not like the authority of those in charge of the institutions of the dominant culture. Jesus tells his disciples who are jockeying for position, "The kings of the Gentiles lord it over them; and those in authority over them are called benefactors. But not so with you; rather the greatest among you must become like the youngest, and the leader like one who serves" (Luke 22:25-26).

In 2 Corinthians 4, authority is defined in terms of "ministry" (service, *diakonian*) (v. 1), "Jesus Christ as Lord" (v. 5), and "ourselves as your servants [*doulous,* slaves] for Jesus' sake" (v. 5). The authority of those who steer the church must be under the authority of Jesus the Lord as servants or even slaves. Those who lead have submitted their will to God's will. They lead not for their own benefit or for praise, but for the sake of the reign of God.

Lesslie Newbigin wrote that Christ's authority for mission is given to the church; there are three elements to this authority:

a living community, a tradition of teaching, and the continuing work of the divine Spirit illuminating the tradition in each new generation and each new situation, so that it becomes the living speech of God for that time, place, and culture. (*Truth and Authority in Modernity* [Trinity Press International, 1996], p. 31)

In our visits, we discovered these aspects of missional church authority: a community of multiple leaders, leaders who focus on missional vocation, and leaders who foster missional practices, both new and from the tradition.

Those in Authority Form Missional Community

A central theme of the Gospels is Jesus' choosing, calling, preparing, and commissioning a company of people. Christ intended for authority to reside in a number of persons taking responsibility to continue his ministry beyond his death. First Corinthians 12 indicates that each person in the church has been given gifts for the common good, and persons with any of these gifts are to work together. Ephesians 4:11-16 mentions the particular gifts with authority "to equip the saints for the work of ministry, for building up the body of Christ" in truth and love, so that all can "grow up in every way into him who is the head, into Christ." The gifts of being called as apostles, prophets, evangelists, pastors, and teachers (v. 11) do not appear to denote that one role is superior to another. The passage assumes all of these persons with authority will work together so that each part of the body is "joined and knit together" and "working properly" (v. 16). Virtually all the congregations we visited had multiple people in authority.

In West Yellowstone Presbyterian Church those in authority are in a constant state of discernment and decision making together. Given the cultural flux of their surroundings, they meet together regularly to study, pray, and rely on each other to be faithful stewards of the mission on which God has sent them. In addition, yearly leaders' retreats help to cement collegiality among them. Here they are able to express frustrations, teach each other through their differing gifts, and move toward communal discernment. This collegiality expanded to include the entire congregation as it navigated the changes needed for missional vitality. When we interviewed two established members of the church, we heard open expressions of sadness in losing an accustomed style of worship, and honest frustrations about moving in a new direction. Yet, the underlying attitude was the willing acceptance of the changes for the sake of the entire body.

The missional change processes at Rockridge United Methodist Church were led by a team of people, some ordained, some not. And each Mission Covenant Group continues to need people with visionary, pastoral, and administrative abilities.

One of the most vibrant examples of collegiality among those in authority and the releasing of spiritual gifts in the community is at Spring Garden Church in Toronto. There they have created a permission-giving structure of authority to "let good things run wild." Missional authority is seeded in the soil of the entire community in order to allow dreams and visions to take root. These dreams and visions are given the resources to become reality. This dynamic sometimes produces flourishing flowers, and at times has created only weeds and disappointed expectations. Yet those in authority at Spring Garden see it as well worth the risk.

The churches of the IMPACT cluster in New Jersey find themselves in a very different context. There have been misunderstandings among the various church members regarding mission and vision, as well as the headaches of collaborating with seven distinct congregational cultures. Yet, the leaders have chosen to operate out of their weaknesses and to become vulnerable one with another. They realize that in order to pursue the purpose of God for them, they would need to be vulnerable and committed.

At Holy Ghost Church, there is community among the pastors and elders. While Bishop Corletta Vaughn wields a great deal of authority, she is open to guidance and instruction by others. We met people who had been tapped for training and mentoring for leadership. The church's four or five pastors and the elders have been nurtured like this, as have young people in the congregation. Holy Ghost Church makes use of its on-site Bible college as a training ground for these leaders.

Transfiguration Parish is led by a core of people that includes its priest. Every Saturday this group of people meets for contemplative prayer, Mass, breakfast, and discussion of issues raised by the Gospel reading for that week. In addition, the group of responsibles, the leaders of each fraternity, forms an informal parish council. They go on retreat twice a year to plan for the church as a whole and identify the issues that the church should deal with during the next six months. Because of such committed lay leadership, the people say that if their priest left, the church would still go on. The vision of presence with Christ and with the poorest of the poor is so broadly shared that it is no longer dependent on Father Karvelis.

Larger congregations in our sample, like First Presbyterian Church of Bellevue, have larger groups of leaders. In addition to several salaried pastors, the church has 140 deacons, trained to provide oversight for every household in the congregation. Deacons respond in time of crisis, help new members integrate themselves into the life of the church, and stay in touch with those who are no longer active, but remain members. The session (church council) makes decisions together and also learns together; each meeting of the session involves 45 minutes of teaching time. Pastor Dick Leon is seeking to cultivate a core of leaders who think missionally.

At Spring Garden Church, Pastor John McLaverty deliberately fosters spontaneity in the structures of the congregation. "It is unpredictable," he says, "the Spirit is in this; we're all swept up in this. There is an aversion to predictability. The kinds of people that join the team [he is missional team leader] believe that anything is possible; we're riding this wave." His attitude is contagious in other members of the team.

Leaders at Spring Garden faced difficulty a few years ago with respect to the "Toronto blessing." They addressed the crisis and moved to the point where everybody could say openly where they stood and why. Eventually, John and some of the elders said, We have to make a statement of our position and people have to choose whether they want to be part of this or not. The elders said to John, You write a letter and we'll support whatever you say. But many other leaders had been part of the process that led to the letter.

When we visited Spring Garden, some people had left. But the pastor was cultivating an expectation that the church together would discern how to address the issues that divided them, in a way that contrasted with the culture around them. In fact, there has been a remarkable process that includes everybody. The pastor may write the vision, but it includes everybody's input in much conversation and many meetings.

Those in Authority Focus on Missional Vocation

Leaders of these congregations are carriers of vision. Sometimes they helped formulate the vision and discern missional vocation. But they always carried vision and helped hold people accountable to the vocation to which God had called the congregation. Among those in authority in these congregations was a passion for the mission of God, regardless of how surprising or difficult it appeared to be. The meetings we attended were not focused on good management or effective techniques, but on how well the congregation was centering on its missional vocation. At Rockridge, for example, the energy of those in authority is focused not on meeting individual needs but on developing the mission and ministry of the church, as a community striving to be a faithful incarnation of God's reign.

Sometimes the beginning of discernment of the vision may come from one leader, such as Father Karvelis at Transfiguration, or a small group, as at Rockridge, before the vision is owned by the congregation as a whole. Elsewhere, the congregation as a whole discerns its missional vocation. At the Boulder Church, in the annual ministry discernment meeting called "map making," they ask, What is our ministry? Who are we and what are we about? Within their larger vocation, their ministry plans seem always to include meeting human need and hospitality, welcoming new people into the congregation.

At Rockaway, one of the IMPACT churches, David, the pastor, is a key participant in a process in which the congregation is involved. The missional vision is part of something bigger than himself or the congregation; he is a mediator in the process, implementer, facilitator. The vision is shared just as strongly by a number of lay leaders. His role is seen as one of participation rather than of trailblazing. The process is shaping him just as much as the others. He has committed himself to participatory leadership. He takes ownership of the vision, but in a particular way, with one eye on the tradition and one eye on the commitment to the vision. That is sometimes a precarious path.

The IMPACT pastors have been meeting at least monthly for over four years. In each of their churches, they have formed a small coalition of leaders linked to the consistory (each congregation's governing body). Yet the role of pastor varies from church to church, in large part due to individual pastors' leadership styles. Some are forceful, charismatic leaders (one pastor so much so that his team members insisted he cede some of his control to them!); others are more reflective and nondirective. What unites them is the importance to all these churches of the formation of these teams for leadership, spiritual growth, and discernment.

As leaders shepherd their congregations through the process of discernment, they are full participants with them. They live the story, and they draw others into the story of God's redemptive purposes for the world.

Holy Ghost Full Gospel Baptist Church has been a part of inner city Detroit since 1941. When the automobile industry there took a drastic turn for the worse, the morale of the changing community was low, and tensions among the residents were high. But that did not stop leaders at Holy Ghost Church from moving into this inner-city neighborhood. The presence of Bishop Corletta Vaughn in particular speaks to the clear calling she has for this part of the world, a response to the prophetic word she received in Africa to go and minister to her own "Jerusalem." She and other congregational leaders have modeled identification with the neighborhood by their physical presence there over the past 10 years.

Such wholehearted participation in the missional vocation stands out. Though other churches might have a flashier facade and more members, few match the degree of transformation that Holy Ghost has stimulated in this area. The dedication of its members and leaders to the welfare of its neighborhood at one point made other churches in the area suspect it was a cult. But that attitude has subsided as Holy Ghost's missional authority has grown uncontestable.

Those in Authority Foster Missional Practices

Missional leaders foster missional practices among their congregations. It is not enough for them to lead the congregation in good projects. If the congregation by its life together is to be a sign of the reign of God, leaders will encourage missional practices and hold people accountable for them.

At Rockridge Church, leaders model and promote the covenant lifestyle that they understand to be as faithful to God's reign as possible, until God's will is done on earth as it is in heaven.

At Transfiguration Parish in Brooklyn, Father Bryan Karvelis and the responsibles of the fraternities identify with the poor and marginalized in their midst. He says,

The people who make up the parish have come through incredible suffering, being mostly poor immigrants. They are very poor, living in tenements, paying outrageous rent, working in extremely unjust conditions. The people are absolutely defenseless. The focus of ministry for these many years has been the same: "To be present to God in contemplative prayer, and to be present to people — the poorest of the poor — with heart and soul." We are blessed with many, many poor people.

For 40 years, Father Karvelis has encouraged his parish in Brooklyn to share in this identification with the poor through the teachings of Charles de Foucauld. Foucauld made it his life's passion to become vulnerable as Christ became vulnerable and be fully present with the poorest of the poor in northern Africa. Father Karvelis's personal lifestyle also reflects this identification. He dresses simply; the same pale green shirt with the stitching coming loose on the pocket served him for both Saturday and Sunday the weekend we were there. He has simple accommodations in the rectory he shares with several other men.

He recognizes that his lifestyle contrasts with other clergy and church structures. "Other clergy see the new paganism of the culture, the aging church, and they don't know what to do about it. They get demoralized. The wider church is getting sucked into the 'planned' American busy-ness scene. They are taking no risks. We are taking risks by doing this ministry here. . . . There would be opportunities lost to the gospel if we did not." As a result, Transfiguration as a whole is sharing in this vulnerability.

First Presbyterian Church of Bellevue is in a different yet no less difficult struggle to foster missional practices with their affluence. Though incredibly wealthy, some leaders at Bellevue are beginning to press the point. They want to confront these dynamics of affluence in their midst and are thus striving toward connection with the poor around the world. Bellevue is pursuing such immersions into lives less fortunate. Mission trips to Central America and Russia have become an expected part of the church's mission for young and old, as well as partnership with an inner-city church in Seattle and providing facility space for an alternative school for dropout students. But unlike many other wealthy congregations, Bellevue recognizes that they must move deeper than just programs and short-term missions in order to be ef-

JEFF VAN KOOTEN AND LOIS BARRETT

fective. They must also confront the missional challenges affluence brings in their own hearts. The authority at Bellevue is struggling to embed missional practices that engage their affluence in a balanced yet radically countercultural way.

Through the cultivation of missional practices within the congregation, those in authority foster a missional identity. They say with Paul, "Live according to the pattern we gave you" (Phil. 3:17). "Follow my example, as I follow the example of Christ" (1 Cor. 11:1).

> Jesus provides us with a clear sense of how leadership is to function in our day. Its central focus is to be that same apostolic mandate of leading out a people as the community of the kingdom. The place of leadership is to be at the front of the community, living out the implications and actions of the missional people of God, so all can see what it looks like to be the people of God. (*Missional Church*, p. 186)

Conclusion

Embodying and Proclaiming the Gospel

LOIS Y. BARRETT

"We do not proclaim ourselves; we proclaim Jesus Christ as Lord."

(2 Cor. 4:5a)

"So that the life of Jesus may be made visible in our mortal flesh."

(2 Cor. 4:11b)

"Yes, everything is for your sake, so that grace, as it extends to more and more people, may increase thanksgiving, to the glory of God."

(2 Cor. 4:15)

The community's thought, words, and deeds are being formed into a pattern that proclaims the gospel of the crucified and risen Jesus Christ. As a result, the good news of God's reign is publicly announced. The proclamation is a "word and deed" proclamation; it is not only audible but visible as well. It is *audible* in a proclamation that focuses not solely upon the salvation of persons, or the transformation of individual human lives, but also the transformation of the church, human communities, and the whole human community, history, and creation in the coming and already present reign of God. It is *visible* in, with, and through the quality of a common life that manifests the unique, culture-contrasting good news of the gospel of Jesus Christ.

We could have called it one of the patterns: The missional church is centered on the gospel. In fact, in our initial list of indicators, the first one was, "The missional church proclaims the gospel." The description of that indicator is above. But as we considered this indicator, it became clear that being centered on the gospel was really a description of the whole life of the missional church. All of the patterns are really summed up in the phrase "proclaiming and embodying the gospel."

The Biblical Understanding of the Gospel

In Mark 1:15, the gospel, the good news announced by Jesus, is summarized in this way: "The kingdom of God has come near! Repent and believe the good news." After Jesus' death and resurrection, the church came to understand that this was the gospel of Jesus Christ. In Jesus, the reign of God had come near — in his preaching and teaching, in his healing, and his entrusting himself to God even in crucifixion, and in God's raising him from the dead. Jesus both proclaimed the gospel and, in his person, was a sign of the reign of God.

Furthermore, as God had sent Jesus, so Jesus sent the disciples and gave them the Holy Spirit (John 20:21-22). The ministry of the disciples — and by extension, the church — was like the ministry of Jesus. The church is called to proclaim the reign of God and to be a sign of the reign of God — to speak, to be, and to do. The church is called to proclaim Jesus Christ (2 Cor. 4:5) and to make Jesus Christ visible in their life as the body of Christ (2 Cor. 4:10-11), so that grace may extend to more and more people, and God will be glorified (2 Cor. 4:15).

Beyond the Old Divisions

Is such a gospel outreach — or nurture? Being or doing? Having mostly to do with evangelism, or mostly to do with congregational life? For the missional church, these old divisions no longer make sense. The missional church both *proclaims* the gospel and *embodies* the gospel. It proclaims Jesus Christ to more and more people — and it makes the life of Jesus visible in itself.

If proclaiming the gospel by word and deed were all that were required to be a missional church, we could write a book on technique: five easy steps to the missional church. And if the previous chapters are read in that way, then we have not gotten our point across. A holistic gospel involves both word and deed. But it is more than that. To be missional is a matter of the *character* of the church, what the church is, whose the church is. Mission is not just one of many activities of the church alongside Christian education, worship, and so on. Mission describes the nature of the church. Its education will be oriented toward proclaiming and being a sign of the reign of God. Its worship will be oriented toward proclaiming and being a sign of the gospel. Participation in God's mission in the world will permeate the whole life of the congregation.

The congregations in our sample used not only "doing" language, but "being" language to describe themselves. "We *are* Matthew 25," said a member of Transfiguration Parish in Brooklyn. Families are encouraged to put signs on their doors, "*Somos* la gran familia de la Transfiguración," "*We are* the big family of Transfiguration." At Rockridge United Methodist in Oakland, they said, "Our first vocation is *to be* the body of Christ."

In a dominant culture that glorifies action and strategies, it is countercultural for a congregation to *be* a sign of the gospel. To be missional is a matter of making Christ visible in the life of the congregation.

Stories of Missional Character

The stories of these congregations speak to their missional character. At the Boulder Mennonite Church, several people told us the story of half the congregation making the tape recording of hymns for the dying child in the hospital. That story said something about the missional character of the congregation.

At Rockridge United Methodist Church, a member named Jim told his story of transformation for himself and another. It involved both proclaiming the gospel, and in the process being changed.

> Seven years ago as I was becoming part of the Rockridge UMC community, I was finishing my master's degree and looking for work as an urban designer and planner.... As our Oakland Discovery Mission Covenant Group began to explore ministry options in Oakland, I volunteered to teach adult literacy at Downs Memorial United Methodist Church. I was assigned to work with Lupe, a woman slightly older than me who was a struggling single mother trying to finish her GED.
>
> At the same time, God was working on me — through covenant group, prayer times, group Bible studies, and retreats. I was beginning to see new life, healing, and forgiveness in my own life and in the lives of others who were in covenant with me.... For the first time, I was experiencing God as a real, tangible presence. After tutoring and encouraging Lupe for a year and a half and attending her graduation, we helped her get established in a pre-nursing program at Merritt College. By that time, I was sharing more with her about God and encouraging her to join a church. Although she had proved she had strength to succeed with a small helping hand, the obstacles she was facing ahead were almost insurmountable. I was beginning to see that the most empowering thing I could give her was a hope and trust in God.
>
> The same was true for my own life, and I felt more than ever the need to solidify my trust and faith through prayer and obedience. My covenant group was crucial in this time of keeping me accountable to the disciplines and praying with me when I needed help. God showed his faithfulness in my job and in our mission, and I was eager to see more of what the Holy Spirit could do to renew the city if we trusted in its power. Now, with the new Community Builder MCG, I am growing with new covenant partners as we seek to serve this city.

What was inner transformation for Lupe and for Jim? What was outer transformation? What was proclamation? What was embodiment of the gospel? Inner and outer were not only connected; they were congruent. What happened in Jim's proclamation was congruent with the gospel's embodiment in Jim and his Mission Covenant Group.

Susan Ortman Goering, co-pastor at Boulder Mennonite Church, related a story about her congregation, in which many people were more comfortable with embodiment of the gospel than its proclamation:

> People who grew up in the Mennonite church have a hard time expressing [their faith] verbally. They take it for granted that everyone has a community and a faith and a place to celebrate. Others in the congregation know that it's not always that way. Ann grew up in an atheistic, dysfunctional family. She has a younger sister who is 32 or 33, still living at home; the sister was 30 when she got her first real job. I said to Ann, "How did you get out of that?" She said, "God sent me my husband, and God sent me to this church." She invites people all the time. She says, "Why wouldn't I tell people?" She has a sense that not everybody in the world has this.

Ann's observation of the embodiment of the gospel in the Boulder congregation became her proclamation to others.

Both these congregations, like the others in our study, are letting the gospel shape the church, often in surprising ways. The gospel is becoming both audible and visible as it transforms individuals and congregations.

The stories in this book are not intended to be imitated. These are not necessarily "successful" congregations. The aim of these churches is not "church-centered mission," where everything is measured by "church growth." Instead, these are "mission-centered churches," focused on the gospel of Jesus Christ. They see the church as an instrument of the reign of God and a witness to the in-breaking reign of God in the world. They want to invite others to enter that reign, so that "grace, as it extends to more and more people, may increase thanksgiving, to the glory of God."

We tell these stories of churches with a missional character so that you may be inspired to let the gospel of Jesus Christ more and more shape your congregation. We tell these stories "so that we do not lose heart."

Appendix

Method

WALTER C. HOBBS

J ust how did we go about this project? Some readers may want to know all the nuts and bolts of the work; others are probably less interested in what we did than in what we found. The following discussion, therefore, is located here in an appendix so that the person who cares to see the detail can find it easily, and others need not be distracted by surplus information.

This study was not "research" as that term is used technically in the social sciences. It was not our intention to generate or to test or to extend theory, whether missiological or congregational or theological. Initially, to be sure, we did conceive it in such terms. We were the Developing Congregational Models research team, one of several such groups in the comprehensive project of the Gospel and Our Culture Network (GOCN) titled "Transforming Congregations Toward Mission." Our charge was to "identify and define tangible congregational models of, and resources for, implementing a missional understanding of the church." As we engaged our task, however, our objectives and therefore our strategies underwent major change.

Early on we recognized that neither the name of our team nor the charge we had accepted suggested we were to construct a model of the ideal missional congregation. Much less had we been asked to tell a waiting world how to go about birthing such an assembly. In discussing what we ought to be doing, we gradually realized that all across North America God was moving congregations in missional directions.

We found that we were regaling one another with anecdotes describing the surprise and delight people expressed as they discovered that their own impulses were shared by many others. Circumstances varied considerably among the congregations whose experiences we recounted — so, too, their vocabularies, ecclesial traditions, and program emphases. But something significant was afoot. We decided we could best fulfill our assignment by gathering stories of the Spirit's activity among such congregations and passing them along to others.

Our hope is that, as these stories are told and perhaps retold, other congregations will be encouraged to begin or to continue their own journeys — different people in different settings with different challenges and different opportunities, but singular in their desire each to be the Body of Christ where the Spirit of God has placed them.

The churches whose stories we tell make no pretense of being models to be emulated. The reader would be ill advised to call any of them to arrange a visit in order to "see how it's really done." They all (*we* all) are simply clay jars. To be sure, they each hold, in greater or lesser degree, mind-boggling treasure. For the present purpose, however, it is critical to keep in mind that the treasure is held in *clay* jars.

As it grew clear that our emphasis should be to offer encouragement to congregations by providing narratives of the remarkable ways in which God is shaping missional communities around the continent, it also became clear that we needed a mechanism by which to recognize churches whose stories should be told. Such churches would reflect in great measure the scriptural imperatives discussed in the work of GOCN's Ecclesiology Project, *Missional Church: A Vision for the Sending of the Church in North America,* by Darrell Guder et al. (Grand Rapids, Mich.: Eerdmans, 1998).

This revised understanding of our task, however, surfaced new issues about method. We had presumed that social science research models would guide our methods. Even there, we faced serious problems. Our individual research competencies had been developed in diverse professional fields. The team includes two professors of missiology, a denominational executive and journalist, a church planter, a cultural anthropologist, a church consultant, and an organizational sociologist and lawyer. Nearly all hold doctoral degrees, and none is a stranger to the research process. But obviously our individual research has been carried out in rather different disciplines with very different research methods, vocabularies, and objectives. At times our conversations had more the character of ships passing in the night than of investigators on a common quest.

Happily, two members of our team examined *Missional Church* closely and then drafted a set of 12 attributes that one might observe in a congregation pursuing *missio dei* (see below). Following a bit of fine-tuning, the (deeply grateful!) team adopted the set of indicators to use as clues, or pointers, for identifying missional congregations. The indicators were expressly *not* intended to serve as tests or gauges or measures of the missional character of any given church. Rather they were to help us notice elements in a congregation's life that would lead one to want to hear more about the journey on which the church had embarked.

We provided the list of indicators to persons we knew were familiar with various churches across North America, hoping we might glean from their observations and recommendations a list of congregations that might be visited. The request was a bit more burdensome than we realized. Numerous colleagues graciously extended themselves in an effort to be of assistance, but the collective responses left us with a set of possibilities too homogeneous than we sought for our purpose. It was necessary for us to pool our own individual experiences in order to assemble a sample as diverse as our time and financial resources would permit us to visit. We focused on diversity with regard to geographic location, theological heritage (Reformed, Anabaptist, Pentecostal, et al.), organizational age, and size. Although it was not difficult to reach a consensus on which congregations should be included if possible, it did develop that upon further inquiry we decided to exclude some congregations. Either new information came to light that cast doubt on their missional commitments, or it proved impossible to schedule a mutually convenient time for a visit. At last, the sample of churches described in the text emerged. It will be obvious to the reader that the sample reflects only a narrow slice of all the congregations of God's people across North America. Sooner rather than later, one would hope, additional inquiries such as this will tap still more diverse congregations, augmenting the stories to be told and the lessons to be learned.

Four churches were visited first, each by a different set of two members of the team. We requested (with varying degrees of success) that any materials the respective hosts might consider informative to us be sent prior to our arrival. On the basis of what we had read, and using the aforementioned indicators as our framework, we interviewed as wide a variety of individuals and groups as time permitted. Some of these persons we asked to meet; others were suggested by our hosts. As early as we could, the team reconvened upon the last of those four visits to discuss what we had learned both substantively and with regard to method. In the remainder of the visits we modified our approaches in light of what we had learned the first time around.

Each visit involved a three- or four-day weekend with the church. We requested opportunity to interview, if possible, founding members of the congregation, participants in the current core leadership of the church, staff members, and new congregants. It had been our hope to meet people in the churches' surrounding communities to gain a sense of each congregation's reputation and impact on its local area, but typically that did not materialize. We sat in on committee meetings and attended Bible studies, kinship groups, and extended prayer times. We were often invited to participate in social events. We attended staff meetings, workshops, Bible school classes for all ages, and a meeting of a fraternity of Transfiguration Parish. We joined our hosts in worship, and we observed them in their ministries to others.

No pair of team members visited more than one church. To the extent possible, we assigned, for each church to be visited, one team member who was quite familiar with the doctrinal heritage represented in the given congregation and another member who would come to the task with fewer (or at least different) preconceptions. Once more the team convened to share our several observations and to discuss one another's insights and assessments in the context of the *Missional Church* framework. These conversations significantly reshaped some of our earlier reasoning about the nature of missional congregations. In particular, our focus shifted away from the supposed attributes or characteristics of such churches, to *patterns* that could be detected in their lives as congregations. Two such patterns that had not been anticipated in the initial draft of indicators received chapter-length treatment in the text. One is "Dependence on the Holy Spirit" (see Pattern 6); the other is "Missional Authority" (Pattern 8).

A comment about the nature of our plenary gatherings: Typically we met for two-and-a-half or three days at a conference facility operated by Divine Word International (a Roman Catholic missionary order) in a northwest suburb of Chicago. On the first day of each session we always took considerable time to bring each other up to date concerning our respective ministries, to describe recent developments in our professional work, and to speak of any joys or challenges that had arisen in our personal lives. As one can imagine, we laughed a lot, and at times we wept together as well. At the start of every day, we studied the Word together, we prayed with and for one another, and we worshiped our God (occasionally, though not always, with song). Regarding each passage of Scripture to which we turned, we asked: How do we read this? How does this read us? How does that impact the work to which we've been called? It was during such a study that we chose the phrase from 2 Corinthians 4 to be the title of our report, *Treasure in Clay Jars*. Among other passages we explored were Exodus 19; Numbers 6; Job 4; Psalms 90 and 135; Isaiah 49; Jeremiah 30; Daniel 2; Haggai; John 15 and 17; Acts 17; Ephesians 3; Philippians 2; and Revelation 5; 20; 21.

The structure of the book itself is faithful both to the title of the work and to our hope that the stories told herein will encourage congregations of God's people to persist in their missional calling. The portraits of each church we visited are intended simply to enable the reader to picture, in some small measure at least, the varied circumstances in which *missio dei* is being engaged. The meat of the report, however, is to be found in the chapters which are based on our understanding of the missional church, God's design for the people of God.

Writing both portions of the book was a collective exercise. The portraits of the churches were initially drafted by the team members, of course, who had made the given visits. These were discussed by the group and revised accordingly, then collected into a single chapter by one of the team. The remaining chapters were spoken for by members who wished to provide the first draft. Those drafts were discussed (that means thoroughly and rigorously critiqued!) by the team *in toto*, and revised and redrafted several times over. In an unusual approach certainly for multiple-authored works and even for edited works, each chapter is a peculiar product of one individual's effort substantially modified by input from six other colleagues. The group then unanimously asked of Lois Barrett (whose many competencies include considerable journalistic skill) that she pull it all together as our editor.

The finished work is not, to repeat ourselves, is *not* a research report. It ought instead to be seen simply for what it is, one more story — no, a few more stories — that we have probed and questioned using our own continually emerging understanding of the missional church in the long history of God's gracious dealings with God's people. What we offer here is a fresh account of the Spirit of God at work today, still dispensing treasure of incalculable worth through the medium of fragile, though often beautiful, clay jars.

Indicators of a Missional Church

A Working Document of the
"Developing Congregational Models" Team

The *Transforming Congregations Toward Mission* Project
of the Gospel and Our Culture Network

Preface

The missional church represents God in the encounter between God and human culture. It exists not because of human goals or desires, but as a result of God's creating and saving work in the world. It is a visible manifestation of how the good news of Jesus Christ is present in human life and transforms human culture to reflect more faithfully God's intentions for creation. It is a community that visibly and effectively participates in God's activity, just as Jesus indicated when he referred to it in metaphorical language as salt, yeast, and light in the world.

The following indicators are an effort to identify what might be some of the key aspects that contribute to the church's unique saltiness and yeasty nature in the varied and diverse worlds within our North American culture today. Twelve indicators are summarized below with a brief definition followed by a statement of "what each indicator looks like" when it is present in a congregation. Each of the indicators is then explained more fully in the subsequent pages.

1. The missional church proclaims the gospel.

   What it looks like: *The story of God's salvation is faithfully repeated in a multitude of different ways.*

2. The missional church is a community where all members are involved in learning to become disciples of Jesus.

   What it looks like: *The disciple identity is held by all; growth in discipleship is expected of all.*

3. The Bible is normative in this church's life.

   What it looks like: *The church is reading the Bible together to learn what it can learn nowhere else — God's good and gracious intent for all creation, the salvation mystery, and the identity and purpose of life together.*

4. The church understands itself as different from the world because of its participation in the life, death, and resurrection of its Lord.

   What it looks like: *In its corporate life and public witness, the church is consciously seeking to conform to its Lord instead of the multitude of cultures in which it finds itself.*

5. The church seeks to discern God's specific missional vocation for the entire community and for all of its members.

   What it looks like: *The church has made its "mission" its priority, and in overt and communal ways is seeking to be and do "what God is calling us to know, be, and do."*

6. A missional community is indicated by how Christians behave toward one another.

   What it looks like: *Acts of self-sacrifice on behalf of one another both in the church and in the locale characterize the generosity of the community.*

7. **It is a community that practices reconciliation.**

   What it looks like: *The church community is moving beyond homogeneity toward a more heterogeneous community in its racial, ethnic, age, gender, and socioeconomic makeup.*

8. **People within the community hold themselves accountable to one another in love.**

   What it looks like: *Substantial time is spent with one another for the purpose of watching over one another in love.*

9. **The church practices hospitality.**

   What it looks like: *Welcoming the stranger into the midst of the community plays a central role.*

10. **Worship is the central act by which the community celebrates with joy and thanksgiving both God's presence and God's promised future.**

    What it looks like: *There is significant and meaningful engagement in communal worship of God, reflecting appropriately and addressing the culture of those who worship together.*

11. **This community has a vital public witness.**

    What it looks like: *The church makes an observable impact that contributes to the transformation of life, society, and human relationships.*

12. **There is a recognition that the church itself is an incomplete expression of the reign of God.**

    What it looks like: *There is a widely held perception that this church is going somewhere — and that "somewhere" is a more faithfully lived life in the reign of God.*

The Indicators in Detail

1. The missional church proclaims the gospel.

What it looks like: *The story of God's salvation is faithfully repeated in a multitude of different ways.*

The community's thought, words, and deeds are being formed into a pattern that proclaims the gospel of the crucified and risen Jesus Christ. As a result, the good news of God's reign is publicly announced. The proclamation is a "word and deed" proclamation; it is not only audible but visible as well. It is audible in a proclamation that focuses not solely upon the salvation of persons, or the transformation of individual human lives, but also the transformation of the church, human communities, and the whole human community, history, and creation in the coming and already present reign of God. It is visible in, with, and through the quality of a common life that manifests the unique culture-contrasting good news of the gospel of Jesus Christ.

Church members indicate that they understand that "proclaiming the gospel" is the responsibility of all Christians; it is more than the vocational option for a selected minority.

Persons are able to point to and articulate the source from which the good words and deeds of the church emanate, that is, in their own words, they are able to indicate, "it is because of the saving gospel of Jesus Christ that you see all these things."

Persons, in their words and actions, express to others what God has done in the world and in their lives through Jesus Christ.

There is evidence that this is a community that can be entered into as a concrete expression of the gospel's own living story. That is, persons can see a community of people who believe, struggle, doubt, sin, forgive, and praise — together.

The body of people admittedly seeks to believe and behave in ways that conform to the gospel of Jesus Christ.

2. **The missional church is a community where all members are involved in learning to become disciples of Jesus.**

What it looks like: *The disciple identity is held by all; growth in discipleship is expected of all.*

Persons are not expected automatically to know the "way of doing things in the reign of God." Citizenship in the reign of God is learned. The learned protocol involves primarily those behaviors and processes that witness to the way of Jesus, who is forming his people for life in the reign of God. The community does not simply rely on "how we've always done things here," or "that's how we Baptists/Lutherans/Presbyterians/Methodists/etc. do it," or even "that's how we do it in the company where I work." Rather, the community seeks critically to integrate already learned practices with skills and habits of Christian discipleship. This community shows evidence of growing, changing, and deepening the skills and habits of discipleship. Nurturing citizenship in the reign of God is an overall priority of the church for all members of the community of faith.

New participants in the community indicate that they are being helped to integrate their life with the practices and habits of life in the reign of God.

Existing participants in the community indicate that they are engaged in a lifelong process of integrating their life with the practices and habits of life in the reign of God.

Illustrations can be given of how people are learning how to pray and are discovering prayer as a powerful resource for living in the reign of God.

The community demonstrates a variety of ways in which participants train, mentor, or nurture one another as the community seeks to develop, across the entire spectrum of participants, the capabilities (ways of thinking, perceiving, and behaving) required of disciples who are attempting to follow Jesus Christ.

Members can identify several different ways of thinking, perceiving, and behaving that are characteristic of life in Christ that differ significantly from the ways of the culture in which persons find themselves on a daily basis. They can give at least two or three examples of how those differences are being practiced in the life of the congregation. (Examples might include rejection of competitive and coercive ways of interaction, use of language that expresses a Christian worldview, attitude toward money and possessions that reflect God's generosity and abundance, exercise of power through service rather than domination.)

The church organization is characterized by the participants as one that is ever open to change, to new and expansive ways of organizational thinking and behaving that enable rather than block the cultivating of faithful discipleship.

3. **The Bible is normative in this church's life.**

What it looks like: *The church is reading the Bible together to learn what it can learn nowhere else — God's good and gracious intent for all creation, the salvation mystery, and the identity and purpose of life together.*

There are two commonly held expectations: that we will seek to know the Scriptures, and that we will seek to become obedient to the Word that is revealed in the Scriptures. Listening, reading, studying, and obeying the Bible is integral to all of church life, including its worship, spirituality, service, education, stewardship, and witness. The Bible is engaged communally. The overarching approach to Scripture study in the body is not solely "personal devotion" or merely "moral guidance," but is characterized by the question, "What is the text saying to the church that is attempting to be faithful today?" "How does the biblical word prepare God's people for their mission in this particular place?"

The community gives visible evidence that its life, work, witness, and worship are influenced and shaped by what the community is learning together from Scripture's revelation of God's claim upon its life.

The community has established processes through which it reflects critically on its hearing of the gospel, and its obedience to the gospel's imperatives, in order to become a more faithful disciple community.

The community is becoming "bilingual" as it learns how to translate the biblical message into the language and experience of its immediate context.

4. **The church understands itself as different from the world because of its participation in the life, death, and resurrection of its Lord.**

   What it looks like: *In its corporate life and public witness, the church is consciously seeking to conform to its Lord instead of the multitude of cultures in which it finds itself.*

   Discipleship requires a willingness to follow the way of the cross and share in the sufferings of Christ. The church is not getting its bearings by the world's standard of success — institutional status, power, or influence. Rather, it witnesses to the truth of the gospel that the one on the cross is the way, the truth, and the life for the church. Jesus models what the church is called to be. Thus the church is called to show hard evidence that as a body of people it provides a collective witness to its crucified savior. The church's distinctive conduct, then, is frequently different from and often in opposition to the world's patterns of behavior. This is particularly evident when the power of love, service, and sacrifice for one another in the community is contrasted with the powers of hate, violence, and domination in the world.

   Members can readily give at least two or three instances when the church was willing to take risks, suffer, be looked down on, or be treated unjustly for the sake of the gospel.

   The church practices love, sacrifice, and service in such a way that people from both within the church and in the wider community can point to their positive results.

   The church is becoming aware of, confessing, and turning away from its patterns of conformity to the world while it learns to follow Jesus Christ.

5. **The church seeks to discern God's specific missional vocation for the entire community and for all of its members.**

   What it looks like: *The church has made its "mission" its priority, and in overt and communal ways is seeking to be and do "what God is calling us to know, be, and do."*

   The goal of decision making is not simply to discover the will of the community, but to discern together the will of God. Because all participants in the body participate in decisions that affect their life and mission together, shared power and influence (rather than status, position, or "majority opinion") are the keys of authority. The need for the gifts and insights of all members to shape and guide a faithful and effective ministry is recognized and empha- sized. Mentors, teachers, and partners provide intentional support, challenge, and advice to enable one another to extend these skills and habits and deepen their participation in the life of Christ. Members make efforts to set aside the necessary time to listen, study, share, struggle, pray, and plan together as they search for God's will and seek to participate in God's mission. Members pledge to live out together the conclusions they have reached to- gether. Church leadership encourages, guides, teaches, and serves the process of communal discernment through consistently hold- ing the following key questions before the community as they seek together to answer them:

> What is God calling us as this church to be and do?
> How can we enter more faithfully into the reign of God?
> How will we learn from the Bible what it means to be the church?
> How will we more faithfully and effectively practice Christian community in our life with one another?

Believing that the Holy Spirit gives gifts to all, the entire com- munity participates in programs and processes for identifying, commissioning, and utilizing the gifts of both new and continuing participants for service in the mission of the church.

The church intentionally develops the skills and habits of lis- tening, praying, studying, thinking, sharing, disagreeing, confront- ing, planning, working together in ways that build up one another, discovering and supporting the rich diversity of giftedness within the community.

Leadership teams and groups demonstrate, model, and culti- vate in their words and behaviors with one another what the whole community is called to be and to do. They indicate that they recog- nize that they too are an expression of the church when they gather, and thus are also intentionally learning the practices of the reign of God in their life together.

6. **A missional community is indicated by how Christians behave toward one another.**

What it looks like: *Acts of self-sacrifice on behalf of one another both in the church and in the locale characterize the generosity of the community.*

The church exhibits the fruits of the Spirit which include (but are not limited to) not thinking more highly of oneself than one ought; valuing the gifts of others; loving one another with mutual affection; eagerness to show the workings of the Spirit; patience in suffering; hospitality to strangers; blessing those who do not understand, or who persecute; associating with the lowly; not repaying evil for evil, but overcoming evil with good; and living peaceably. Acts of generosity are commonplace and self-giving is a behavioral characteristic of this community.

Congregational life demonstrates a variety of ways for cultivating the attitude and habit of expressing self-sacrificing compassion and concern for one another.

The church exhibits patterns of individual and corporate prayer which seek to promote the welfare of the community as well as the transformation of lives and changed conditions within their locale.

There is indication that the church is changing its expectations about what participation in the Christian community looks like (for example, spending more time with one another, taking their relationships with one another more seriously, providing tangible support for one another).

7. **It is a community that practices reconciliation.**

What it looks like: *The church community is moving beyond homogeneity toward a more heterogeneous community in its racial, ethnic, age, gender, and socioeconomic makeup.*

The barriers that separate people are identified, addressed, and overcome. Differences and dissension among people are dealt with constructively. Conflict is used to enrich discussion. Evil done within or to the body is overcome by doing good. Healing involves confession to and the forgiveness of one another wherever and whenever wrong exists. This process of healing and reconciliation takes place between individuals and within the body, both of which serve to shape and reform the community as a whole. Society's boundaries are crossed — class, economic status, race, gender, age, occupation, education. Amazingly diverse people allow themselves to be formed by one Lord into one body. Violence is rejected as a method of resolving difference.

Members can give anecdotal evidence from the church community life showing where forgiveness and the healing of relationships occurred — consistent with the life of Jesus and in contrast to the society's standards of behavior.

There is evidence that leaders and members expect positive results from expressing differences.

There are norms by which the community abides for the constructive use of conflict. These include informal or formal procedures of which both leaders and members are aware and can make reference to.

There are examples of reconciliation that indicate the community is learning to transcend racial, ethnic, age, gender, socioeconomic barriers. The community values and accepts both similarity and difference out of its unity in Christ.

8. **People within the community hold themselves accountable to one another in love.**

What it looks like: *Substantial time is spent with one another for the purpose of watching over one another in love.*

They covenant together to uphold and watch over one another in love, praying for one another. They are committed to one another, and that commitment is expressed through collaboration, interdependence of work efforts, and being dependable. People place a high value on sharing a common life and supporting one another.

Participants indicate that a fundamental purpose of the community is the expression of Christ's love — mutual love and accountability to one another.

Participants indicate that they are accountable to a grouping of people with whom they are learning to live the Christian life more faithfully. (In such a grouping, they are learning to acknowledge their status as forgiven sinners, receiving from and giving both encouragement and admonition to one another, helping one another to live in God's grace, seeking consistently to be restored to right relationships with one another.)

Participants indicate that the community is characterized (i.e., it is the norm rather than the exception) by a life together carried out in a unity of spirit. Consistently, words and actions toward one another indicate mutual respect for one another.

Participants take time to pray for one another. They pray for one another in their varied circumstances, circumstances that are not limited to sickness or death. They pray for those with whom they differ and whom they dislike as they do for those with whom they agree and whom they like. They recognize that prayer is a key aspect of being accountable to one another in this community.

The community reflects on how its structures (meetings, frequency, length, and use of time together, organizational structures, physical arrangements) either hinder or enable the demonstration of mutual love, respect, and accountability to one another.

9. **The church practices hospitality.**

What it looks like: *Welcoming the stranger into the midst of the community plays a central role.*

People are reached and invited into new relationships with God and with one another as the community's intent is to welcome as God welcomes. As a result, people are becoming citizens of God's reign. Having heard and received this invitation themselves, they extend the invitation to others to know and experience God's love.

The church demonstrates a sense of urgency about inviting people to enter the reign of God.

Visitors experience welcome, aid, and comfort, thus making

wider the circle of the church community to include those who are different from us.

10. **Worship is the central act by which the community celebrates with joy and thanksgiving both God's presence and God's promised future.**

What it looks like: *There is significant and meaningful engagement in communal worship of God, reflecting appropriately and addressing the culture of those who worship together.*

Worship is the community's action of publicly giving allegiance to God — Father, Son, and Holy Spirit. It is an act of the whole people of God who remain faithful to tradition while integrating variety that reflects and gives new meaning to the unique cultural context of the congregation. Worship actively engages the community in ways that nurture the dynamic, growing, and changing aspects of discipleship in the world. As such, it provides for the incorporation of people into the community of faith, their formation into a new humanity, and their reception of God's gift of sustenance for daily life. Its focus is on celebrating God's presence and promises without seeking or expecting worship to be the occasion for God to meet human needs. The congregation departs from worship, knowing that it is a sent and sending community, and each Christian is conscious of his or her apostolic sentness as light, leaven, and salt in the world.

The organization, structure, content, language, rituals and practices of worship demonstrably focus upon God and give opportunity for human responses to God.

There are aspects of communal worship that reflect the local culture, but also give new meaning to those elements of local culture.

Participants can give anecdotal evidence of how corporate worship enables persons to become incorporated into the life of Christ, and thus the Christian community.

Participants can describe ways in which worship gives expression to and provides the experience of God's sustaining presence in the life of the congregation.

11. This community has a vital public witness.

What it looks like: *The church makes an observable impact that contributes to the transformation of life, society, and human relationships.*

What the community intends to be and do actually does occur, and is confirmed both by those who participate in the community (e.g., "I have learned here that I can disagree and I don't have to leave") as well as by those who do not (e.g., "Oh, you're the church that always helps clean up after floods and tornadoes"). Like political ambassadors, persons know and can articulate where their allegiance lies. They know and can articulate the nature and expectations of the mission that has been given to them. Its public deeds do not consist of imposing its moral will on others, but of giving hard evidence of the reign of God that intrudes as an alternative vision and practice.

The community defines itself as "sent" — representative of the reign of God and offering alternative ways of life to the world, where participants know themselves to be accountable to one another and to God for the faithfulness of their witness in daily life.

Members of the local neighborhood and/or larger church can give examples which illustrate a variety of actions through which the church, over time, has communicated God's love in the immediate locale and elsewhere.

Members can identify examples of actions and activities that have resulted in the transformation of lives, changed conditions, promoted justice, and combated evil (e.g., economic injustices, violence, discrimination, addiction, oppression).

12. There is a recognition that the church itself is an incomplete expression of the reign of God.

What it looks like: *There is a widely held perception that this church is going somewhere — and that "somewhere" is more faithfully lived life in the reign of God.*

The church has been given the gift of citizenship in the reign of God which it has received less than perfectly. Knowing that the church is as yet a flawed witness to the reign of God, it is open to its own reformation as it continually seeks to provide a more faithful and more effective witness in its changing context. Therefore, the church is constantly critiquing and intentionally reshaping its vision, common life, teaching, organization, obedience, witness, and ministry on the basis of its hearing of the Word of God.

When people talk about their church, there is evidence of honest review of its ministry and mission, measuring itself against biblical standards of the reign of God, and not culturally established standards of success.

The measure of success used in this church is the quality of Christian love experienced in its common life and ministry.

People who participate indicate that this church is on a journey to the future, that it has not yet arrived.

Participants are able to pray with meaning Jesus' prayer "Thy kingdom come." This prayer creates for them a sense of expectancy and anticipation of God's fulfillment of all God's promises.

This church demonstrates faithfulness, while recognizing that it has not yet fulfilled its calling.

Recognizing itself to be a human institution, the church intentionally seeks evaluation, redirection, and renewal through the Holy Spirit.